The Thai House

The Thai House

History and Evolution

Ruethai Chaichongrak, Somchai Nil-athi, Ornsiri Panin
and Saowalak Posayanonda

Photography by Michael Freeman

First published and distributed in
the USA and Canada by
Weatherhill, Inc.
41 Monroe Turnpike
Trumbull, CT 06611

A River Books Production

British Library Cataloguing-in-Publication Data.
A catalogue record for this book is available
from the British Library.

ISBN 0-8348-0520-0

Editor and Publisher: Narisa Chakrabongse
Design: Holger Jacobs at Mind
Production Supervision: Paisarn Piemmettawat

Printed and bound in Thailand by
Amarin Printing and Publishing (Public) Co., Ltd.

Cover: A Lan Na house in Lampang which formerly
belonged to Chao Mae Yod Kham.
Title page: A scripture pavilion within the grounds
of Wat Luang, Phrae.
This page: Three rice granaries from the North-East.
Overleaf: The sitting room of Suan Pakkad Palace.

Introduction

The Central region and the ruen Thai derm

The traditional Thai house, with its characteristic features of a wooden house on a platform raised on posts and a gabled, elegantly tapering roof has been in existence for many centuries. It appears on Dvaravati stone reliefs from the 8th century and in sketches in La Loubère's Chronicles, which were written in the late Ayutthaya period. Other foreigners such as the Abbé de Choisy in the 17th century and Sir John Bowring in the 19th century also mentioned houses on posts lining the banks of the Chao Phraya river.

These houses are known as *ruen Thai derm* or the traditional Thai house and are among the most beautiful wooden houses found in Southeast Asia. Architecturally they represent the perfect response to Thailand's geographical and climatic conditions. The high platform and spacious terrace is well-suited to the tropical climate which combines baking sun and abundant rainfall, often leading to flooding. The use of wood and bamboo reflects the once abundant natural resources, while the modular system of pre-fabricated wall panels and gables erected on site was suitable for a country where land was abundant and houses could be moved easily.

As a predominantly agriculturally-based society, the lives of Thai people were closely integrated with their environment, a relationship which, over the centuries, has led to the development of many customs and beliefs, which are closely bound up with the lifestyle of the people and their homes.

Diverse forms and traditions

It would be a mistake, however, to imagine that Thai houses are the same throughout the kingdom. Regional differences are extremely important and can be seen in such features as the choice of materials, pitch of roof, layout of the interior, etc. Function also plays a significant role and thus many different forms of the basic house have evolved – the riverside raft house, the stem family's clustered houses, the shop house, houses for monks and rice-field shacks. The effect of time and fashion must also be taken into consideration as houses in all the regions have undergone a continuous process of modification in terms of their functions, aesthetic preferences and construction techniques.

While the classic Thai traditional house is very much associated with the Central region, the distinctive geographies, climates and cultures of the three other main regions – the North, the North-East and the South – are reflected in their vernacular architecture.

In addition, with all the four regions an important distinction exists between the larger wooden houses (*ruen krueng sab*) of the relatively wealthy and the vernacular house, built of bamboo (*ruen krueng pook*) or a combination of bamboo and real wood. The vernacular house has a gabled roof with thatched palm leaves or grass, a floor of flattened bamboo (*fark*) or wooden planks, and walls of split bamboo or thatched grass. The *ruen krueng pook* are used for other structures such as granaries and barns, or for rice-field shacks.

Above: A line drawing by a western artist of a traditional Thai house from the Ayutthaya period. (From *A Description of the Kingdom of Siam* by De La Loubère)

Opposite: A library from Wat Rakhang Kositaram which is where King Rama I lived before he became king. Formerly it was two Thai houses facing on to a central terrace. Later when it became a library the open terrace was roofed over. It is a classic example of an early traditional Thai house of the *khahabodi* style.

During the the reign of King Chulalongkorn (Rama V) much of Thai life was still located on the river or canal. Small boats were used for transportation and buying and selling.

Northern Thai houses

The north of Thailand forms a district region very different from the Central plain. Geographically the area is dominated by mountain ranges and four main river valleys running roughly north-south, while the climate is significantly cooler. Known as Lan Na, until the 19th century it was not fully integrated with the rest of the country and over the centuries it has developed its own cultural and architectural traditions.

Certain unique characteristics distinguish Lan Na houses from those of the Central region. The terrace of Northern houses is not in the middle with rooms leading off and the verandah is usually at the gabled end of the house compared with running along the length in the Central region. To cope with the colder climate in winter, the houses have small windows and extended eaves which sometimes come down very low. The entrance stairway is covered and has a *raan naam* (a small shelf for water containers) at its head. The kitchen is usually built to the front of northern houses and to the side or the back in Central region houses. The *panlom* or windbreak finial of Central Thailand is replaced by a *kalae* – a pair of carved wooden boards crossing one another at the top of the gable as decoration. The houses do not have any *yong* (carved panels under the windows) but instead have special carvings, *hamyon*, over the bedroom doors to protect the inhabitants. In addition to the spirit house, there is also a small house for the ancestor spirits.

Above left: Habitations along the canal were diverse. They might be on dry land, be raft houses or boat houses.

Above: Roadside shop houses in the *ruen krueng pook* style have walls of the *khat thae* type. They are not raised as high off the ground as ordinary houses.

Opposite: The interior of the lacquer pavilion at Suan Pakkad Palace. This structure dates from the Ayutthaya period and is one of the few examples to have survived. The scenes from the Life of the Buddha, in gold and black lacquer, take place within a naturalistic setting which shows the architecture and daily life of the period.

Opposite: A *kalae*-style house on Talad Chin Road in Lampang. It is typical of the *ruen krueng sab* type of northern domestic architecture.

Right: The characteristics of a *toob yao* house. (The Museum of Isaan Houses, The Institute for Herbal Research, Maha Sarakham University)

The North-East: Isaan traditional houses

Isaan, or the North-eastern region, is a relatively arid area with a low annual rainfall. Although once widely covered with dry deciduous dipterocarp forests, most of the area has suffered heavy logging. The region is also subject to frequent flooding caused by tropical storms originating in Laos, Cambodia and Vietnam. The average annual income of Isaan people is lower than the rest of the country. These physical and economic limitations are reflected in the simple forms of Isaan houses, which are built mainly to satisfy the basic needs of the occupants, and have less carvings and other decorative details when compared with the houses of the other three regions. Roofs are frequently covered with grass thatch or corrugated iron rather than the more expensive terracotta tiles. The more elegant houses in Isaan are found along the banks of the Mekong river where there is an abundant supply of water for domestic and agricultural use and the people are better off economically.

Nevertheless, the simpler houses situated in villages or in the middle of rice fields have a stark beauty, and the traditional customs and beliefs regarding all aspects of family life including house construction are extremely interesting. Like elsewhere, Isaan houses are raised high above the ground to cope with the annual floods, leaving the area beneath the house for resting, weaving, spinning and other handicrafts, as well as sometimes being used for animal enclosures.

Above left: An example of the crossed eave extensions known as *kalae*. These carved gable ends are one of the defining characteristic of Northern Thai, or Lan Na architecture.

Above right: A model of a *kalae* house with a triple-gabled roof.

Right: The front elevation of a typical Thai Muslim house.

Bottom: Intricate roof details and finials on the gables are characteristic of Thai Muslim houses.

Below: A double-gabled Thai Muslim house with two sets of concrete steps. The house posts are concrete in order to deal with the heavy rainfall.

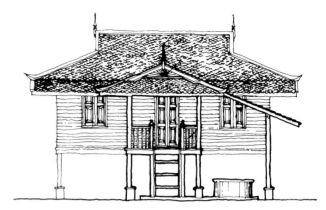

Traditional Southern houses

The Southern region is composed of a long peninsular with the Indian Ocean to the west and the Gulf of Thailand to the east. Its geography and its greater proximity to the Equator means that the region has a more humid climate and constant rainfall throughout the year. The main occupations of the region include fishing, mining, rubber growing, trading and agriculture.

The area has a heterogeneous population whose different occupations, belief systems and ethnic origins have led to a significant degree of architectural diversity. Unlike the rest of Thailand where Buddhism is the principal religion in the South Islam plays a prominent role with some 70% of the population of the four southernmost provinces being Muslim.

A combination of these cultural and geographical characteristics is reflected in the house forms, which vary according to the functional requirements, religious beliefs and physical locations. Characteristic features of houses in the region are the hipped roof, often with gables and elaborate roof decorations as well as the raised floor on posts some 1.2-2 metres high, resting on stone or concrete footings to prevent decay caused by frequent rains. The intricate fretwork carving which adorns both exterior and interior wall panels, not only provides ventilation but is an important decorative feature. In addition, the decorative details are often brightly painted, a practice not found elsewhere.

Above: A Thai-Muslim house with a *blanor* roof belonging to Kamnan Abdul Rormekator, Yarang district, Pattani province. The top of the pediment is decorated, while the windows are curved on top and have coloured glass. The central window extends from floor to ceiling, a feature known as *pitunatae*.

Right: A cluster of houses with a *blanor* style roofs, Bajoh district, Narathiwat.

Chapter 1
The Central Region

When people speak of a traditional Thai house, they generally have in their mind's eye an elegant, wooden panelled house on high posts with two or more buildings clustered around a central verandah through the centre of which grows a large, shady tree. Underneath the house may stand an ox cart, some agricultural implements and a low table on which the owners and their friends sit and chat. Within the compound are a variety of fruit trees such as banana, durian, coconut, pomelo and lime. A buffalo may be tied to a fence post. The house might be situated on the banks of a *klong* (canal) or river, or on the side of the road. As well as tending the fields, the family might also trade from their house.

Today such houses still exist but they are becoming hard to find. Often corrugated iron has replaced the traditional tiled roof and various additions have been tacked on any old how. Or, if recently built, they may serve simply as a stylish adjunct in the grounds of modern compound, or be the setting for a restaurant, where Thais or foreigners can come and savour for a while the delights of natural wood and beautiful proportions. In fact, many Thais do not appreciate them, finding them dark or poorly insulated and ill adapted to modern cities. For hundreds of years, however, they were the perfect dwelling. Standing in the midst of shady trees, near the owners rice fields, they used locally available materials, they were prefabricated and could be moved and re-erected. Raised high above the annual floods, they were also cool and breezy and, above all, beautiful.

Before we look at the house in detail, let us turn to the wider context in which they were situated. In the past they were not an isolated anachronism in the midst of a dusty city, but an integral part of a village community, embodying ancient beliefs and a way of life that has almost vanished.

Thai Villages

Ribbon-type villages along river and road

Physical environments are important determinants of human settlement everywhere. Early Thai settlements tended to originate near canals and rivers because the livelihood of their inhabitants depended mainly on water for domestic and agricultural use as well as for communication. Riverside villages are common features along most waterways. The first word of their name is usually *bang* which means a village settlement or group of shop houses built along a canal or river, or on the sea coast. Examples of this type of village are Bang Ya Praek, Bangkok Noi, Bang Hua Suae, Bang Plama, Bang Prakok and Bang Plasoi.

After a group of houses had been built, other essential facilities such as a market and a temple would soon appear. In the past the market was the centre for the exchange of goods, at first through the barter system and later through the money economy. The need for a permanent trading centre led to the emergence of a riverside community, which subsequently expanded in a linear formation along the waterway. Situated immediately behind a riverside village would be the fruit orchards and behind that the fields for rice and other crops. Linear expansion made it difficult for a riverside village to develop an efficient administrative unit. However, once the village had prospered a temple would be established as the community centre. Riverside villages which grew so large that distinct boundaries were delineated by protective moats and earthen

mounds, were referred to as *muang ok-taek*, or a divided city, the name being derived from its characteristic feature of a waterway running through the town. A classic example of such a 'divided city' is Suphan Buri.

Before the advent of the car and bus, people used elephants, horses and bullock or buffalo carts to travel along inland roads. The speed of land travel was restricted by the animal's stamina. On a long trip, it was normal to make an overnight stop to rest the animals. People who lived nearby would bring their products to trade with the travellers at these stops. Some of the most frequented stops later developed into permanent settlements with shop houses replacing the temporary huts. Trading was carried out in the front of the shop houses while the back provided living quarters. Like riverside villages, the fruit orchards and rice fields lay behind the houses of the roadside villages.

Cluster-type villages

Villages also developed in areas away from any canal or river. As a rule this type of village was usually located on high ground above the rice fields. The villagers would build their houses in a single cluster and worked in the outlying fields on the edges of the community. There was a large communal water pond for domestic use in each village, with the main rains and annual floods, which arrived between the 11th and 12th lunar months, providing the water for agricultural activities such as the transplanting of the rice seedlings into the

Above: In the past goods traded between different centres were often carried on long poles resting on the shoulder.

Previous page: A Central region house from the King Rama II Memorial Park in Samut Songkhram province. Note the *kamyan* (truss) supporting the extended eave.

Above left: An aerial photograph showing the siting of houses in Suphan Buri province on slightly elevated ground to avoid flooding. The word '*don*' or '*bang*' meaning raised was often incorporated into the name of the village.

Above right: This photograph shows the dense concentration of dwellings along rivers and tributaries. Access to water was important for all aspects of Thai life, both domestic and agricultural.

Right: A group of traditional houses whose roofs still use elephant grass as a thatching material, Muang Boran, Samut Prakan province.

Right: Shops were erected along the canal and buying and selling was conducted both on land and from small boats.

Below: An aerial view showing a loose village arrangement where each house is surrounded by rice fields.

Below right: Boats have been used for transport for many centuries. Wooden bridges have been constructed across this *klong,* or canal, at Damnoen Saduak so that market traders and their customers can move about freely.

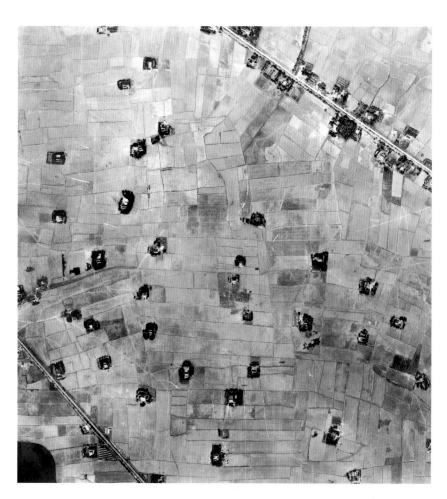

flooded fields. The names of villages in this category normally begin with *Bang* or *Don*, such as Bang Sa Yai Som, Bang Pong Larn, Bang Tham Kradarn, Don Klang, Don Manao, Don Chedi, etc.

Loose villages

This type of village would grow out of an alliance of many isolated houses scattered among their own fields over a large area. These houses may originally have developed from rice field huts. Their physical isolation prevented villagers in such associations from developing a close-knit community based on social, cultural and kinship ties like villages in other categories. They remained loosely united.

Above: A group of raft houses, reconstructed at Muang Boran, accurately capture the flavour of life along the water's edge.

Far left: A typical double-roofed house as would have been used by a farmer. (Muang Boran, Samut Prakan province)

Left: A spirit house. Such miniature dwellings are always built in the house compound to house the spirits who had been displaced by the building of the main house. Food and offerings will be made by the owners.

Types of Traditional Thai Houses

The way in which the different components of a traditional Thai house are arranged relates closely to the family structure.

A nuclear family single house

This type of house forms a family residence for a husband, a wife and their unmarried children. It has a *ruen norn* (sleeping unit), a kitchen, a *rabieng* (verandah) and a central *charn* (terrace). The *ruen norn*, between six to nine *sork* wide (a *sork* being a Thai unit of measurement equivalent to the span of an adult's elbow) and 15 to 18 *sork* long, consists of a bedroom and an open hall. The *ruen norn* is a three-post span structure: one span is used as an open hall, while the other two are reserved for the bedroom. The hall houses the altar for the Buddha image. A covered verandah is added to the area in front of the bedroom, connecting the latter to the terrace. It is generally used as a living area. The kitchen is a two post-span structure connected to the *ruen norn* by the central terrace, with the first post-span for cooking and the second span for dining.

The *charn* or terrace, connecting the sleeping area to the kitchen, is an outdoor living area, while the terrace behind the kitchen is for bathing and washing.

A stem family clustered house

A nuclear family becomes a 'stem family' after one of the children gets married. It is a Thai custom for married men to live with the wife's family as it is believed that this will cause the least conflict between the two families. Nevertheless, at this stage the one bed room house becomes too small to accommodate the new son-in-law. Extending the original house would entail a lot of work as the existing walls and floors have to be taken down and re-attached. In addition, there are various taboos relating to adding to or adapting an existing building. As a result, the family frequently opts for the building of a separate house next to the old one. This also ensures a degree of privacy and freedom of movement for all members of the family.

The new house is built opposite that of the parents, with the gabled ends facing in the same direction. A kitchen is then added to the back of the existing *ruen norn*. Another unit can then be built opposite the kitchen and adjacent to the sleeping quarters later on. The walls of the new house are usually filled in on three sides, leaving the side adjacent to the parents' terrace open to be used as an additional living area for resting, receiving guests and organizing religious ceremonies. The bedroom of the original house can also be extended to three post-spans by adding partitioning panels to the hall area.

To summarize, there are three different ways of adding a new *ruen norn*: building new quarters parallel to the parents' house; forming a cluster house by building new quarters connected by the communal terrace; or building separate quarters in the same house compound with no connecting terrace.

Above: Khun Paen's house at Ayutthaya province is a classic example of a traditional cluster arrangement.

Right: A traditional house belonging to Dr Lek Tantasanee which uses a combination of *fa samruad* (bamboo) and wooden panels. The eaves are supported all around the house by *kamyan*. Bonsai trees are grown in pots, a style of plant decoration very popular with the owners of traditional houses.

Above: The bird pavilion at the home of the late Mom Rajawongse Kukrit Pramoj, former Prime Minister and author of a classic of Thai literature, *Four Reigns*.

Right: An aerial view of Ruen Ton.

Above: Ruen Ton shows the cluster arrangement typical of a *khahabodi's* family. This beautiful group of houses was built by King Rama V in 1904 as a place where he could relax and entertain in an informal setting. It consists of several houses clustered around a large open verandah. A wooden panel separated the two large halls into one for the men (the so-called front area) and one for the ladies (*fai nai*, the inner area).

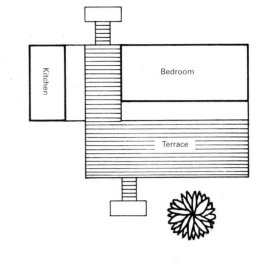

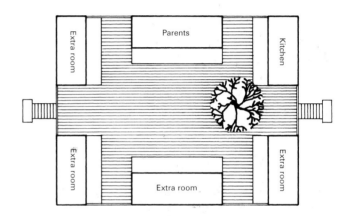

Ruen khahabodi (a wealthy family house)

Wealthy people built larger and and more elegant types of clustered houses which would normally consist of the following structures:

The *ruen norn*, forming the main house of the group, is usually the largest with the width of eight to nine *sork*. The *ruen loog*, or minor house, is opposite to and smaller than the *ruen norn*. The *ruen khwang*, the crosswise house, may also be called the *ruen klang* or *hor klang* (central hall). This structure has only three walls, the fourth next to the verandah being left open as a living area where the occupants come to rest, receive guests, have meals, organize religious ceremonies and other social functions like a top-knot cutting or weddings. It is the equivalent of the *hor chan* (dining hall), or *hor suadmon* (prayer hall) in the *kuti*, or monk's residence. The open, three-post span structure is situated at right angles to the *ruen norn*. It may or may not be situated in the middle of the terrace, depending on the direction of the *ruen norn* and the available space.

An overly large *hor nang* or *hor klang* can be a problem as seen in the Khun Paen house, a replica of an old existing clustered house, in Ayutthaya. In the original cluster, the *hor klang* was built as a minor structure whereas in the replica it is designed to be the central structure. As a result, the new *hor klang* has been enlarged to dominate the other structures in the group and, thereby ruined the spatial flow, which gave

Above left: A model showing the roof structure of a typical Central region Thai house.

Right: Traditional Thai houses can be grouped in various ways. The top shows a simple arrangement of *ruen norn* and kitchen for a single family. Below it are two different plans showing how they can be enlarged to cope with the development to a stem family.

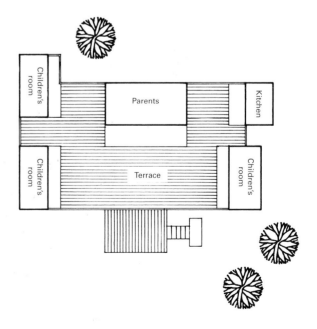

Ban Moh palace is situated within the old city moat in Bangkok and was built by Prince Phitakthewet, who was a son of King Rama II in 1832. This palace shows how a classic Thai house can be enlarged and adapted.

Left: An altar for Buddha images is found in every Thai house. This set of altar tables at Ban Moh palace is simple but elegant, flanked with two ivory tusks on both sides. Pictures of the ancestors of the present-day owners hang on the wall.

Right: The throne hall, with various cabinets and tables in carved and gilded wood. The monk's pulpit and fan can be seen at far left. In the background, may be seen the door in Chinese style, which was very popular at that time.

Below: Another view of the throne hall showing several low Thai tables with carved bases and legs.

such a wonderful feeling of movement in the original cluster house design.

The *ruen khrua*, the kitchen, is located to the back and at right angles to the *ruen norn*. It is quite a large structure with woven bamboo matting for wall panels and uncovered gables for smoke ventilation. The *hor nok*, a bird hall, is a two-post-span structure built alongside the *hor khwang* to house the cages of the popular turtledoves.

Normally, the central *charn* (terrace) of a *ruen khahabodi* is very large and designed in such a way that it blends into the natural surroundings around the house. A large flowering or fruit tree, such as *champee* (*Michelia longifolia*), *champa* (*Michelia champaca*), and *chan* (*Dyospyros*), mango (*Mangifera indica*) or breadfruit (*Artocarus altilis*), would be planted in the opening in the middle of the terrace. Fragrant climbers such as canagium and jasmine were grown up one side of the terrace, while ornamental plants in pots were dotted around other areas of the terrace.

Although stem family clustered houses and *ruen khahabodi* are both multi-unit dwellings, their composition and construction stages are very different. Clustered houses originate from a single unit of *ruen norn* and *ruen khrua* which is expanded with the marriage of a daughter. *Ruen khahabodi* are designed and built as a group to provide a more prestigious home. The presence, or lack, of a *hor nang*, *hor nok* and *hor klang* can be used to distinguish the two types.

Above: A collection of planters on the verandah. Apart from bonsais, old-fashioned Thai plants are very popular such as various types of aloe or *tako*.

Right: The bed of King Rama II (r.1809-1824) is elaborately carved and gilded. A Thai-style cabinet shows puppet heads. (Mom Rajawongse Kukrit Pramoj house)

Below right: The sitting area and bedroom in Mom Rajawongse Kukrit's house is divided by pierced wooden panels.

Opposite: A sitting room within the house of Chan Chaem Bunnag. The low table in the centre can be used as a writing desk. Thai cabinets house books and files. This house shows how a traditional building can adapted to modern life.

Opposite: A large room within the Jim Thompson Museum, used for receptions, is decorated with traditional Thai furniture and antiques such as Buddha images and scripture cabinets.

Right: The verandah outside one of the houses in Mom Raja-wongse Kukrit's compound has a European style spiral-post cabinet containing Sawankhalok ceramics, a lion-footed Thai cabinet with puppet heads and a third displaying Benjarong china (a five-coloured glazed porcelain much favoured in the 19th century by the royal family and courtiers).

Bottom right: The *charn* of the traditional Thai house at the Rose Garden resort, Nakhon Pathom province, has been with roofed over to give additional covered space.

Left: The study in Mom Raja-wongse Kukrit's house has gold lacquer Thai-style bookcases. To the left is a lion-footed low table on which stands a minia-ture howdah.

Below left: A low carved and gilded table supports a Burmese-style Buddha image in the Jim Thompson Musuem.

Below right: A shrine room in the house of Chan Chaem Bunnag. Behind the principal image is a *satthaphan* – a long, carved wooden candle holder frequently found in northern Thai temples.

The shrine room in Mom Raja-wongse Kukrit's house contains many Buddha images from different periods of Thai art. There is no ceiling so that the inner structure of the roof is apparent. Traditional Thai houses of wealthy families would always have a separate room for the Buddha images and family relics.

Opposite: The dining room of the Jim Thompson Museum. The Chinese table is carved with a dragon. The plates are Chinese porcelain. The walls are hung with Buddhist paintings. The custom of sitting on chairs to eat around a table reflects the western influences which were already apparent during the reign of King Rama IV. It was not typical of ordinary Thai families who have traditionally sat on the floor when eating.

Right: In the background of the sitting room of Mom Rajawongse Kukrit's house is a lion-footed carved and gilded table on which stands a Khmer stone figure of Uma. The display cabinets contain puppet heads and enamel ware. The electric ceiling fan would have been a later addition. In the old days, Thai houses did not need such cooling devices having been designed to take advantage of any passing breeze through the many windows and open floor plan.

Below: The main bedroom within the Jim Thompson Museum is entirely furnished with Thai antiques. The bed base is a large lion-footed table which is carved and gilded. In the past the beds of richer families would be paneled on three sides such as the example on page 30.

Kuti

There is not a rigid distinction in Thai architecture between the styles used for religious and secular buildings. Thus the traditional Thai dwelling was not confined to lay people but was also used to house monks and was also enlarged and adapted for other monastic buildings. Generally, the *kuti* is a relatively small structure in Thai style designed for a single monk. Its confined space helps to discourage the accumulation of material goods, other than those which are permitted. Even food such as salt must be stored in a separate structure called the *kappiyakuti* (a food storage unit apart from the monk's living quarters).

Rule No. 6 of the *Sanghathisek*, the 13 canons of Buddhist monks, states that a monk's *kuti* should be a 12 x 7 *keub* (equivalent to 4.013 x 2.343 m). It is communal property and its location must be chosen and approved by other monks prior to construction. Any *kuti* not conforming to these restrictions are flawed and a violation of the canons. Within these rules, various arrangements of *kuti* are possible.

Urban *kuti* (in Bangkok and its vicinity) share the same composition, floor plan and structural elements of the traditional clustered house, especially the three-room house (*ruen sam hong*). This is not surprising as some *kuti* are, in fact, clustered houses that the owners or their descendants have dismantled and donated to the temples, where they have been reassembled. Buddhists regard this as a way of making merit.

Above: A group of single *kuti* with projecting eaves at Wat Bupparam, Trat province.

Right: A typical layout for a group of *kuti* in a city temple shares many features of a cluster house. As with the secular arrangement, the terrace has openings for trees. Note the scripture store at bottom right.

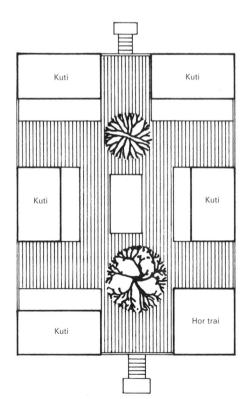

Kuti   Kuti

Kuti   Kuti

Kuti   Hor trai

Above: The scripture house or *hor trai* of Wat Yai Suwannaram in Phetchaburi province was constructed in a pond to protect it from ants. The *chofa* (roof finials) are in the *bai raka* form and the eaves project at the front. Behind this building are the monk's dwellings or *kuti* whose panels are in both *fa pakon* and *fa samruad* style.

Left: Inside the *sala karn parien* or Preaching Hall at Wat Yai Suwannaram. This temple was built in the Ayutthaya period. There are nine pairs of octagonal wooden columns decorated with gold lacquer. The walls show traces of naturalistic murals with trees, birds and other animals. At the far end is a carved monk's throne with gilding and glass mosaic.

Opposite: The interior of a *kuti* in the grounds of Wat Yai Suwannaram being used to house the body of a monk who died while spending the rainy season at this monastery. Buddhist Lent which coincides with the rainy season is a time when monks do not go out on their daily alms round but stay in the monastery.

Right: A group of *kuti*. Note the *kamyan* supporting the caves and the extension at left.

Left: The exterior of the Preaching Hall at Wat Yai Suwannaram, built at the beginning of the Rattanakosin era, has all the hallmarks of traditional Thai architecture such as the roof finials and eave boards. The pediment is carved with a *kranok* design (swirling tendrils). The eaves are supported by trusses, carved as *nagas*, or serpents, at the same intervals as the columns. The panels are in *fa pakon* style. The bottom portion is decorated with large *krajang padiyan*.

Five- and six-bedroom *kuti* are not old houses donated to the temple but are built specifically as monks' residences. This type of *kuti* can still be found in some temples, such as, the four-room *kuti* of Wat Mai Bang Krasorb in Samut Prakan province, or the six-room *kuti* at Wat Chanasongkram, Wat Ratchasittharam and Wat Hong Rattanaram in Bangkok.

Kuti are otherwise arranged in groups or rows, connected by a central terrace with a *hor chan* (dining hall) or *hor suadmon* (prayer hall) in the middle. However, in certain temples this hall may be situated to one side of the *kuti* cluster allowing an open space in the middle for large trees like mango, *chomphu* (*Eugenia jambos*), *champee*, *champa*, jackfruit (*Artocarpus heterophylla*) and *chan* (*Dyospyros decandra*). One order (*khana*) or group of monks usually shares a single *kuti* cluster. The more orders there are in a temple, the more *kuti* clusters, but all must be situated in the *sanghawas*, monks' residential area, of the temple.

A popular arrangement of *kuti* in the provinces is a twin-roof structure similar to a twin house. One section of this is partitioned into a room while the other is an open hall with a terrace connecting both sections at the front. This type of *kuti* provides the monks with a space for resting and receiving both male and female visitors outside their bedrooms. In the provinces the *kuti* of an order of monks are arranged in two rows with the *hor chan* in the middle. The terrace is balustraded on all sides with an opening at each end.

A *kuti* at Wat Hong Rattanaram, Bangkok, is in traditional style with *fa pakon* panels. The roof has projecting eaves. The whole stands on a concrete base.

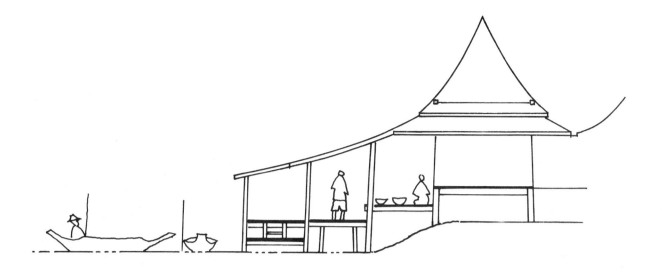

Left: A cross section of a water-front shop showing how it was divided into its various functions: sleeping, selling, storage, walkway, etc.

Below left: Canal-front shops have walkways in front and a series of bridges connecting them to other shops. On the right is a Chinese-style pavilion.

Bottom left: A raft-house arrangement in which three separate houses sit on the same platform. (Muang Boran, Samut Prakan)

Riverside shop houses

In the past much of Thai life was conducted from boats, and even today canals and rivers remain important for transportation, washing, irrigation and fishing. River- or canal-side shops were thus an essential component of daily life. The traditional-style wooden buildings were designed to combine trading and residential use in a single structure which was divided into two sections: the front section for displaying goods and trading, while the back was for family life. The living quarters normally consisted of a hall, a bedroom, a kitchen and dining area, while the nearby canal or river served as a bathroom.

Attached to the front trading section of each shop house was a wooden walkway bridge, one-metre wide, which connected all the various shop houses in the area. Landings, for the loading and unloading of goods, were built either on the same level as the walkway bridge with ladders leading down to the boats, or were at a lower level than the first type with a ladder connecting the two. In some instances, there might be even another lower landing, using 20-40 cm wide planks, constructed at water level or about 10-15 cm below.

Although riverside shop houses look similar to other traditional Thai houses at the back, differences are found in the front elevation. The front wall panels are either folding (*fa na thang*) or upward opening (*fa barn krathung*) panels. The latter style of wall panel is

made of lightweight materials like thatched palm leaves (*fa krachaeng orn* or *fa samruad*) or woven bamboo matting. However, nowadays the folding panels and the upward opening panels have almost all been replaced by wooden folding doors (*fa thang barn luean*) or doors of corrugated iron.

Riverside shop houses are usually built in a single row along both banks of the waterway with small open spaces (one house span) for mooring boats between the houses. Trade is most active before noon when people come in their boats to sell produce such as fruits, rice, vegetables, fish, crabs, prawns, shellfish, and poultry, clothing and other necessities. They return home in the afternoon. People who live in the riverside shop houses have a different lifestyle than those living on land. Most traders have developed extensive trading and social networks. There are different activities going on all day long. As much as half of the space in the shop house, sometimes even more, is taken up with the display of goods, trading and storage, with the latter sometimes spilling over into the residential section as well. The usually indispensable *charn* (terrace) of the traditional Thai house is omitted altogether in riverside shop houses.

The *ruen pae* is basically a shop house on a floating platform, which doubles as a family residence. It is similar in appearance to the traditional twin house; the inner house provides living quarters, the outer one is an open trading area with the front verandah

extended to the water's edge, and, in some cases, there are verandah on both sides. Most shop houses are three-room units with the kitchen and dining area at the back, the kitchen being smaller than the main house. Two types of raft are used to support the floors: *pae loog buob*, consisting of stems of bamboo tied together, and *po*, a rectangular hardwood platform with the interior structure of a boat, caulked with tree resin in order to make it watertight. Each shop house rests on four to five *po*. Both types of platform have to be repaired every year.

The shop house structure sitting on top of the raft is similar to that of a traditional Thai house but its joinery is much more resilient. As with the other land-based shophouse the old style folding or lift up panels have been replaced with folding doors.

Above left and right: Raft houses and fixed houses may have roofs of grass or terracotta tiles.

Below left: The floating market in Damnoen Saduak canal, Ratchaburi province. Produce can be brought straight from the fields and orchards to be sold at canal-side shops.

Above: A 19th century photograph of the Chao Phraya river showing twin raft-houses and house boats. In the background can be seen the *prang* of the Temple of the Dawn.

Top left: This river-front shop has abandoned traditional roofing materials in favour of the more modern and durable corrugated iron.

Top right: A twin raft-house on the Chao Phraya river. On the left of the photograph is the shop part of the construction with an awning for shelter.

Above: Both these riverine scenes show how busy life on the water was in the past. Nowadays the wake generated by long tail boats means that these small paddle boats and raft houses would not be safe.

Right: A cross section of a road-side shop showing the lower platform at the front.

Below: A twin-roofed shop house which although not very old is built in the traditional style.

Bottom: This shop house has a lower, wider verandah than normal with similarly wide eaves in order to give more room for commercial transactions.

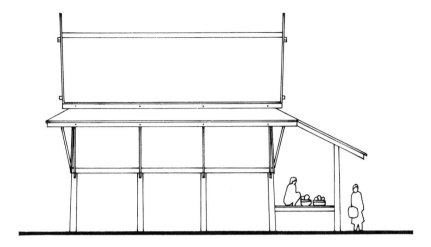

Roadside shop houses

In the past there were many land-based dual-purpose trading and residential buildings which were similar in appearance to the riverside shop houses, although in this case goods were delivered by cart. However, it is difficult to find such shop houses today as most have been dismantled to be replaced by the rows of ugly concrete modern buildings which line the roads running through many Thai provincial towns and villages. Among traditional roadside shop houses it is possible to distinguish four different types.

The basic structure comprises a *ruen norn* with a verandah at the front which is almost the same size. Designed for the display of goods and storage, the verandah is much lower than the main house – less than two *sork* above the ground. The front panels of the shop house are *fa fiem*, *fa than* or *fa khat thae* (the latter opened by lifting upward and being supported with a long pole). There is a cooking area at the side or the back of the *ruen norn*. The open space under the house is used to store the carts.

With a large family, the *ruen norn* is built as a twin house while the verandah at the front is the same as the first type. In the third type, the only difference is that the verandah is situated at the side of the *ruen norn*. In the fourth type, the trading section is an open pavilion completely separated from the *ruen norn*. The goods are displayed during trading hours and put back in storage after the shop closes.

A typical roadside shop in Phetchaburi province during the reign of King Rama V. The photograph was actually taken during a royal visit. Note the roof coverings of *ya kha* grass (*Imperata aundinacea*) or palm leaves.

Characteristics of Traditional Thai Houses

House forms

A traditional Thai house is raised above the ground to a just above head height. The varying levels of the different sections of the house are determined by the different functions and create a flow of space which is almost modern in feel. The highest part is the bedroom floor which is usually about 260 cm above the ground; the next level is the verandah, which is 40 cm lower; and the terrace, which is 40 cm lower still. These 30-40 cm differences in height are also very suitable for sitting with the feet resting comfortably on the lower level, therefore, effectively turning the upper floor level into a bench. In Ayutthaya, Suphan Buri, Ratchaburi, and Kanchanaburi it is customary to build the verandah on the same level as the bedroom floor with only the terrace on a lower level. The loss of seating is compensated for by less construction work, as there is no need for additional beams to support another floor level.

There are many considerations which led to a raised house being highly desirable. Firstly, it provided security from animal predators and thieves at night. The central region of Thailand is situated in low-lying areas inundated by frequent rain and floods. In the past, its forests abounded with dangerous animals such as poisonous snakes, centipedes and scorpions. Houses with a raised floor provide a sense of security, privacy and shelter. Secondly, flood evasion was of primary importance. All regions of Thailand are subjected to inundation during the rainy season, with the floods sometimes lasting for several months. In the northern and northeastern regions flooding comes from rainwater and storms while in the central region it is caused by overflowing rivers from the north and high sea levels in November and December. People, animals and implements can be kept temporarily in the house during the floods.

At other times, the underneath of the house becomes a useful multi-purpose area. It can be used to store agricultural implements like carts or ploughs, timber, boats and large pans for making palm sugar. It also provides space for such supplementary activities as umbrella making, weaving, spinning and rice pounding. The space underneath the house can be used as a living area during daytime. In certain areas, such as in the Song Phinong district of Suphan Buri, the space underneath the house is allocated for livestock and poultry enclosures. However, many regard the keeping of animals underneath the house as unhealthy because it makes the area dirty and foul-smelling. Other provinces prefer to provide a separate space for animal pens close to the house. During the Songkran festival (the Thai New Year which is celebrated on April 13th) in the Phra Pradaeng district of Samut Prakan the area underneath the house is elaborately decorated to entertain visitors. This area can be used as a playground and a working area for such activities as washing and splitting bamboo strips.

Above left: The area under the house can be used for a variety of functions. It is a cool place to rest, store agricultural tools or engage in rural handicrafts.

Above right: A defining characteristic of a traditional Thai houses is the raised floor on posts which protects the house from flooding.

Opposite: A group of houses within the King Rama II Memorial Park, Samut Songkhram province. Although these were only built some 20 years ago, they are excellent examples of traditional Thai architecture. Their location within a coconut grove provides shade and aesthetic appeal.

Right: In a traditional Thai kitchen, food preparation would be done sitting on the floor. Note the many apertures in the wall panels in order to ventilate the room and get rid of any cooking fumes and smells. The floor of the kitchen could be either split bamboo or wood.

Below: A typical Thai kitchen will have utensils such as chopping boards, knives, a stone pestal and mortar, pots and pans, as well as ingredients such as garlic, lemon grass, kaffir limes, and chillis.

A raised house also provides better ventilation than one situated on the ground. Situated between 13-16° N and 95-106° E, central Thailand has a hot and humid tropical climate with temperatures as high as 39.9° in the hot season. The lofty and highly ventilated traditional Thai house is an ingenious adaptation to such a climate.

The kitchen

Thai food is delicious but using garlic and spices leads to strong smells during the cooking process. Thus the kitchen walls need to be well ventilated, hence the open panels which can either be *fa samruad* (split bamboo) or *fa khat thae* (woven bamboo). In some houses even the kitchen floors are made of woven bamboo matting.

The kitchen gables are also designed for rapid smoke exhalation, having ventilation slats in a radiating *rasami phra arthit* (sun ray) pattern, thereby creating an excellent marriage of form and function.

The roof

The roof of a traditional Thai house is a high-pitched gable in the Manila style with extended eaves. The high pitch is necessary to prevent leaking and the wooden structure is covered with palm leaf thatch or terracotta tiles. In addition, the elevated roof lets out the heat from inside the house, ensuring that the interior is relatively cool. Wide lower roof extensions protect the interior from rain and glare.

Above: These high pitched roofs are covered with terracotta tiles. The gable has *loog fak* wooden panels.

Far left: A popular gable end design has the form of a sunburst, which not only reflects the soaring quality of the roof but also gives good ventilation. This one is from the house of Lamai Salipon in Suphan Buri province.

Left: The interior of the roof space of a traditional house.

The terrace

One of the characteristic features of a traditional Thai house is its large, balustraded *charn* (terrace) with takes up almost 40% of the total floor area. If the verandah space is included with the terrace, the ratio of total outdoor area to indoor area will 60% to 40%. Such an emphasis on outdoor space is a an obvious architectural response to the prevailing hot and humid climate.

For a Thai house, a terrace is as essential as the bedroom and kitchen because it provides the much needed ventilation and continuous air circulation. The occupants can look through the terrace balustrades, to the fruit trees surrounding the house and then to the countryside beyond. It is this integration of inside and outside which is a particularly appealing feature of much tropical architecture.

The terrace functions as a multi-purpose open area for relaxing, receiving visitors, organizing traditional functions like the top-knot cutting ceremony, merit making, offering food to the monks and weddings.

Architecturally, it draws the different sections of the house into a single unit. In a clustered house the various units are formed around a central terrace. Open spaces and low balustrades between the houses allow a continuous flow of space. Sometimes large trees are planted in an opening in the middle of the terrace to provide shade and introduce a natural element. Popular trees for this purpose are *chan*, *champa*, *champee*, jackfruit and mango. Other corners of the terrace are

Above: Some terraces are extremely spacious and were therefore used for special events and ceremonies.

Below: Trees were frequently planted in the centre of the terrace to provide shade.

Opposite: The terrace of Ruen Ton is unusual in having a partition. This was to separate the *fai nai* women's quarters from the outside.

Large trees with fragrant blossoms are frequently planted in the terrace openings of Thai houses in order to provide shade and scent. Ornamental planters with bonsai trees are placed around the terrace. (Dr. Lek Tantasanee house)

reserved for decorative plants like *bon* (*Caladieum*), *wan* (various sedges and herbs), *koson* (*Codiaeum variegatum*), *tako dat* (trained *Dyospyros*) and water lilies.

Floor plans

Superstitious beliefs and local aesthetic preferences are more important than strict scientific or architectural principles in the design of a house plan. Most Thais believe that their lives are dependent on both natural and supernatural forces. Contrary to expectations the path of the sun is not a determining factor in house location in the central region. Similarly, neither is wind direction a consideration when drawing up a house plan, as the house design already provides good ventilation and most social gatherings usually take place on the outdoor areas of the terrace or beneath the house which are already cool and shaded.

In general, a riverside Thai house is oriented towards the waterway for easy access. Thus the front, or verandah, side of the house, is parallel to the river or canal, regardless of the direction in which the water flows. When a house is not on the water, its front will be oriented with the nearest road. There is also a belief that houses in the same village should be aligned in the same direction, rather than in an opposite or *khwang* direction, so as to avoid conflicts among the owners. Therefore, the orientation of the very first house in the group will determine the direction for houses built at later periods. This belief still prevails in Don Phai Chong

Lom village in Song Phinong district of Suphan Buri.

In contrast, the ethnic Mon villages of Ban Krachaeng, Ban Song Khanon and Ban Ter follow a different principle by building their houses *khwang*, or at right angles to the river, which flows from north to south. This provides good ventilation as it corresponds to the prevailing wind direction. The term 'Mon *khwang*', an ethnic slur against the Mon, derives from this practice which seems strange to the Thais.

On the stele of King Ramkhamhaeng, found at the ancient capital of Sukhothai, the south is referred to as *tit hua norn*, or the direction in which a sleeping person should point their head, while the north is *tit teen norn*, the direction of their feet. This indicates the existence for many hundreds of years of beliefs regarding the alignment of the body during sleep. The

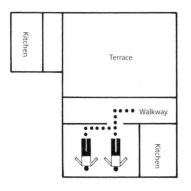 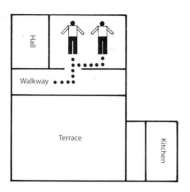 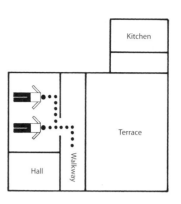 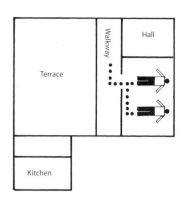

N

Wind direction

direction in which one's head points may also be dependent upon other factors determining the house plan. In addition, there is a taboo against sleeping with one's head to the west, the direction of the setting sun, associated with death and destruction. Thus the heads of dead people, when laid out before cremation, will point to the west. However, although the south is the most desirable direction, there is no restriction against pointing towards the east, considered an auspicious direction. Not only is this where the sun rises, but the Lord Buddha faced east on the day of his enlightenment.

Because several people often share the bedroom, other factors to take into consideration are whether latecomers will disturb those already sleeping by walking in near their heads and whether the sleepers may have to be in two rows.

Above: Four different ways in which traditional houses can be positioned to take account of favourable breezes and auspicious directions.

Example 1: The long side of the terrace faces north. This plan allows for many sleepers to lie across the long side of the house, with their heads pointing to the south, the correct direction. Because their feet point towards the door, they will not be disturbed when other people enter the room. Air flows through the whole length of the room from south to north. Both morning and afternoon glare cannot reach the terrace, making it suitable for resting, while the hall receives good ventilation.

Example 2: The terrace is positioned to face south. Many sleepers can still be accomodated but they may be disturbed by latecomers if they point their heads to the south.

Example 3: The terrace faces east. Fewer sleepers can be accommodated if they sleep with their heads pointing in the most desirable southwards direction, or more if they sleep in two rows, but this is unsatisfactory because the feet of those in one row are near the heads of those in the second row. If the sleepers lie across the length of the room their heads must point to the east and latecomers will disturb them.

Example 4: The terrace faces west with the sleepers pointing their heads to the east and their feet towards the door and walkway. There is good ventilation in the bedroom, but not in the hall and the terrace gets the afternoon sun. From these examples it becomes apparent that the best arrangement is one where the long side of the terrace faces north, followed by that where the terrace faces west.

Below left: A typical bedroom within a Central Thai house has a mattress on the floor and very little furniture, apart from a small dressing table.

Right: Between the terrace and the bedroom of Ruen Ton there is a high threshold with a step provided to enter the inner room which is on a higher level.

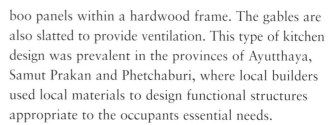

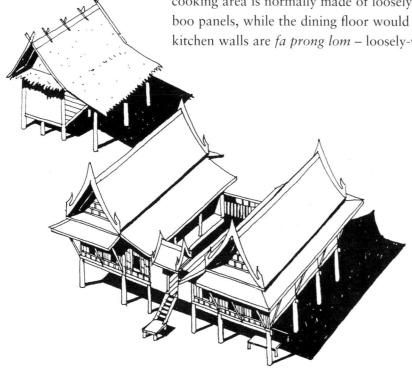

The kitchen floor plan

The kitchen of a Thai house is normally built as a separate structure from the *ruen norn*. The fact that firewood and charcoal, which cause much smoke and grime, are used for cooking necessitates that good ventilation is a top priority in any kitchen. This results in the characteristic design of slatted kitchen walls and gables, a feature which distinguishes it from the *ruen norn*. In general, the kitchen is a two post-span structure with the cooking area occupying one of the spans and a dining area the other. The floor of the cooking area is normally made of loosely woven bamboo panels, while the dining floor would be teak. The kitchen walls are *fa prong lom* – loosely-woven bamboo panels within a hardwood frame. The gables are also slatted to provide ventilation. This type of kitchen design was prevalent in the provinces of Ayutthaya, Samut Prakan and Phetchaburi, where local builders used local materials to design functional structures appropriate to the occupants essential needs.

To conclude, the plan of a traditional Thai house is based on adjustment to the physical environment rather than on scientific principles relating to the trajectory of the sun or the prevailing wind. It is usually aligned lengthwise to be parallel to the nearby road or river. Superstitious and supernatural beliefs are the most important factors in drawing up the plan of a Thai house.

Structural characteristics

A traditional Thai house is a prefabricated and portable structure, which can be assembled and dismantled in the following order: the main house, the kitchen, and the terrace. All the components are wood, mainly teak, although woods such as *teng* (*Shorea obtusa*), *rung* (*Shorea siamensis*), *daeng* (*Myrtaecae*) and *makha* (*Afzelia xylocarpa*) are used for certain components, which require exceptional strength. A Thai house is essentially a post-and-beam structure, the gravitational forces being transmitted from the roof to the ground through the *klorn* (rafter), the *pae* (purlin), the *jantan* (rafter), the *sao* (post), the *kongpat* or *rae* (a piece of wood nailed to the bottom of the post to prevent it

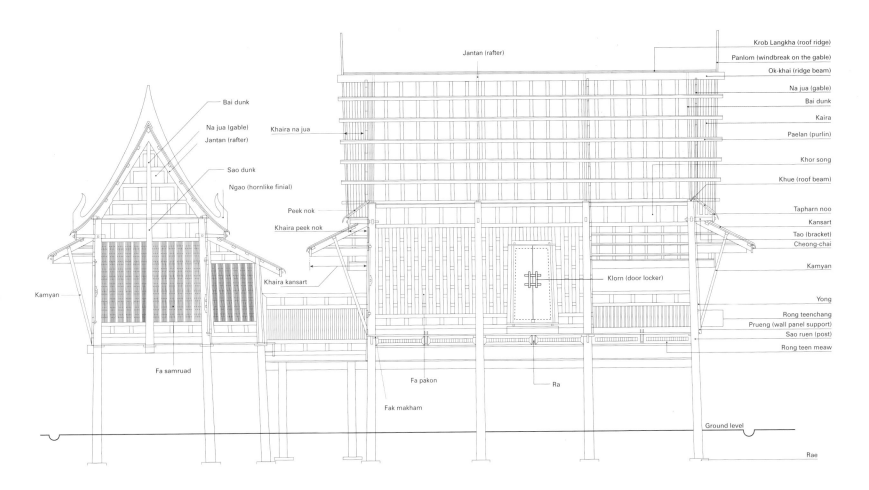

Krob Langkha (roof ridge)
Panlom (windbreak on the gable)
Ok-khai (ridge beam)
Na jua (gable)
Bai dunk
Kaira
Paelan (purlin)
Khor song
Khue (roof beam)
Tapharn noo
Kansart
Tao (bracket)
Cheong-chai
Kamyan
Yong
Rong teenchang
Prueng (wall panel support)
Sao ruen (post)
Rong teen meaw

Jantan (rafter)

Bai dunk
Na jua (gable)
Jantan (rafter)
Sao dunk
Ngao (hornlike finial)
Khaira na jua
Peek nok
Khaira peek nok
Klorn (door locker)
Khaira kansart
Kamyan
Fa samruad
Fa pakon
Ra
Fak makham
Ground level
Rae

Above: Major components of a Central region house.

Left: This group of traditional-style houses by a Bangkok canal was built recently. Some traditions are respected but there are adaptations for modern life – the posts are concrete, the terrace is tiled and the *hor nang* has glass windows with air conditioning.

Opposite: Inside Tamnak Daeng or Red Mansion, the former residence of Queen Sri Suriyendra, the queen of King Rama II. The house stands within the compound of the National Museum. In the foreground, is a corner of the Chinese-style bed. In front of the bed is a low table for sitting and receiving female guests.

from sinking). A Thai house tapers inward which means that the floor area is wider than the space at the top on all sides (a form which is achieved by loosely attaching the top ends of the posts to the roof crossbeams before jerking the bases of the posts outward). A wider base has various benefits. Firstly, it confers structural strength and stability by increasing pressure on the tops of the posts. The inward tapering house frame, like a person standing with legs apart, is more resistant to vertical forces than a straight frame.

Secondly, it helps in attaching the walls. When the wall panels are raised on the *prueng* (a rectangular wood frame used to brace the house floor and walls) they will automatically lean against the tapered posts making it possible to secure them with only four Chinese-style nails. The tapered wall panels also apply more weight to the structural elements making them more stable. The verandah of a Thai house can be built on the same or at different levels to the bedroom and the terrace floors. When built on different levels additional beams are added to support the extra floor. There are two techniques for adding multi-level floor beams. One is to attach new beams to the existing posts and the other is to plant extra posts, as high as the desired height of the new floor, about 50 cm away from the old posts to support the new floor.

The *charn* (terrace) is a structure built separately from the main house and the kitchen on posts planted approximately 50 cm from the main house posts.

Top: The verandah of Plai Noen palace has a long bench for receiving guests and sitting and chatting.

Above: This *kuti* in the grounds of Wat Kongkaram in Ratchaburi province has a row of subsidiary columns which support the eaves. The windows are carved and inlaid with glass mosaic.

Regional Characteristics

Slight differences among traditional Thai houses can be observed in the different provinces that make up the Central region. Such differences may relate to the aesthetic features, to construction and joinery techniques, to certain structural components or to beliefs concerning the construction procedure.

For example, houses in Kanchanaburi (those that have *kansart* or extended eaves), Nakhon Pathom, Samut Prakhan and Petchaburi are similar in their well-proportioned structure, refined workmanship and lavish components. Nevertheless, it is possible in Kanchanaburi to find houses both with and without *kansart*. Those without are noticeably less elegant in form and inferior in workmanship. While most houses are similar in size, a large house with a roof cross beam of more than eight *sork* has been found in Don Chedi sub-district of Phanomthuan district. It is a house of exceptional width and excellent proportions.

In Nakhon Pathom, the houses are of equally fine proportions and excellent workmanship as the Kanchanaburi house. Ruen Tap Khwan is a magnificent example of a *ruen khahabodi* and a masterpiece of classical Thai architecture.

Houses in Samut Prakan are noted for their exquisite wall panelling of the *loog fak* type. In addition, they have a complete set of traditional Thai house components. Their floorboards are laid along the length rather than the width of the house. The floors are laid on 5 x 5 cm *tong* (joists), which are placed on the

rawd (floor beams) at 30 cm intervals. Examples of these houses are found in Ban Song Khanong, Ban Ter and the *kuti* of Wat Mai Bang Krasorb. About 40 years ago, all the houses in these villages had no fences and the children could wander through all the houses at will, as most families in the villages were related by close kinship ties.

In Phetchaburi, the houses have *fa pakon* (patterned wood panel) walls with *kansart* (extended eaves) and elongated *panlom* (windbreak on the gable). Another unique feature of Thai houses in this province is the use of *fa samruad* (split bamboo) walls, which have particularly closely spaced vertical and horizontal teak battens not found elsewhere. In contrast, the *fa samruad* in Ayutthaya, Pathum Thani, and Samut Prakan have vertical bamboo battens mixed with horizontal wooden ones. Houses in both Phetchaburi and Samut Prakan are built with the same level of excellent workmanship.

In Nonthaburi and Pathum Thani, the houses are similar in style to the ethnic Mon houses in the Phra Pradaeng village of Samut Prakan. However, the Mon houses are more interesting, displaying great expertise in making wall panels of the *fa pakon kradarndun* and *fa loog fak kradarndun* type, compared with the more common types of panelling. A unique feature of houses in these two provinces is their orientation along a north-south axis, which is characteristic of the ethnic Mon house.

Above left: This house in Kanchanaburi is eight *sork* wide which is exceptionally wide. It also has *kansart* and is thatched with nipa palm.

Above: A Suphan Buri house of the type with no *kansart* or overhanging eaves to protect against the rain along the sides.

Far left: This Suphan Buri house is well-proportioned and constructed using *fa pakon* panels. However corrugated iron has been used for the lower eaves.

Left: Houses with *fa samruad* panels are rare nowadays.

Below: The walkways and verandahs of this group of Thai houses was built by Ruethai Chaichongrak at Mahidol University.

Above: On either side of the porch over the steps at Ruen Tap Khwan are pierced panels for ventilation. It was built by King Rama VI.

Right: Ruen Ton is typical of the more wealthy traditional house. The floor is rather high and there are many units arranged around the central terrace. There is a waterfront pavilion at left.

Left: Khun Paen's house in Ayutthaya is a cluster house comprising a central unit, side units and transverse units. In the middle of the house is a large hall known as the *hor nang* which is somewhat oversized (*see line drawing below*).

Below: A drawing of Khun Paen's house.

Bottom: A large group of Thai houses have been built in the Institute of Anthropology at Mahidol University. They stand on concrete footings in a lake.

In Suphan Buri, there are two styles of houses. Firstly, those with all the components associated with a traditional Thai house, including wall panels of the *fa pakon* type and very high posts to cope with flooding. The second type lack the *kansart* or extended eaves to protect the house from the tropical sun and rain. Nearly 50% of traditional Thai houses in Suphan Buri lack such eaves and, consequently, suffer from rain and sun damage. In addition, their form is also less attractive. Originally, most houses were built with extended eaves but when these were destroyed by windstorms they were not replaced.

In Bangkok, Chachoengsao and Nakhon Nayok, the houses are reasonably elegant and of good workmanship. Variations in quality will always be found, however. Thus if two groups of cluster houses both built by kings are compared, the workmanship and proportions of Ruen Tap Khwan in Nakhon Pathom are far superior to that of Ruen Ton.

In Ayutthaya, as in Samut Prakan, there are two types of houses but the variations are different. The first type, of which hundreds still remain, has high pitched roofs with elongated gables, and are generally of uniform quality. The walls are mostly *fa pakon* wooden panels and the roofs are adorned with *panlom* as well as *ngao panlom* (a horn-like finial). The second type has low-pitched roofs and fishtail-like *panlom*. The kitchen walls are *fa khat tae* panels in teakwood frames while other walls are wooden *fa pakon*.

A central terrace can often provide the largest uninterrupted space of the whole complex. Its function is a multi-purpose one: access to the various units, a place to sit in the shade of a central tree or to receive visitors. This example is from Ruen Tap Khwan, Nakhon Pathom.

Traditional Beliefs

In the past, superstitious and magical beliefs played a significant role in the lives of Thai people. Many persist to this day such as beliefs in astrology and in the need to choose auspicious times for conducting important activities including house construction. Specialists in these matters are usually astrologers and monks who are knowledgeable in magical, astrological and Brahministic beliefs. There are a number of taboos and proscriptions connected with house construction.

In the provinces of Suphan Buri and Phetchaburi, animist practices are still performed by the ethnic Song and Puan groups with the offering of foods and other materials to the spirits of the land, the house, etc. Beliefs related to house construction are mostly animistic and magical in origin and are quite elaborate. Although there are certain regional differences regarding such beliefs, in practice, people tend to follow fairly similar principles and procedures for house construction. The fundamental principles of house construction cover various aspects from choosing an auspicious location, to selecting suitable materials and moving in at an appropriate time.

Selecting the site

In the selection of a suitable house location a divination involving an animal is required, in this case a crow. A divination based on the same principles may be seen in the Royal Ploughing ceremony, in which the weather and annual rice yields in the coming year are interpreted from the types of food chosen by the ceremonial bulls. In a divination ritual for a suitable house location different white, red and black rice grains are set out in the chosen house location for the crows to pick from. If the crows choose the grains of red or black rice, it is a bad omen and the location is deemed unsuitable. The house owner then has to look for a new location and repeat the divination process.

Another method for selecting a site is by scent. Lumps of earth from a prospective site are sniffed for their aroma. If the soil smells of the *pikun* (*Mimusops elengi*) flower, the site is auspicious and is referred to as *saptri-phumi*. If the soil has the scent of the lotus and *matulee* flower, it is also auspicious known as *promma-phumi* that will bring wealth to the occupants.

Auspicious times

Six months – the third, fifth, seventh, eighth, tenth and eleventh lunar months – are proscribed as it is believed that they will bring suffering and disease. In contrast building during the first, second, fourth, sixth, ninth and twelfth lunar months will bring happiness and good fortune. Days of the week can also be auspicious or inauspicious. Saturday, Sunday and Tuesday are auspicious, while Monday, Wednesday and Thursday are inauspicious. Friday is considered to be neutral and it is believed that houses built on this day will bring their occupants an equal share of happiness and misery.

Above: A spirit house based on a traditional cluster house. Such buildings are found throughout Thailand and are the abode of the spirit of the place who protects the inhabitants of the main house.

Opposite: This colourfully decorated double-gabled spirit house stands on the banks of a canal in Thonburi. Inside are a pair of male and female spirit dolls symbolising the spirits of the place. Their attendants sit on the balcony, while small dancers are in the courtyard below. Marigolds are an auspicious flower.

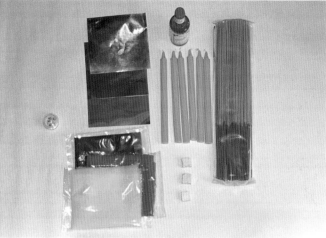

Far left: Before construction can begin the *berk na prom* ceremony must be performed. This involves cutting a small slit at the centre of the inner side of the gable.

Left: Some of the items which are used during the ceremony to install the house posts: candles, joss-sticks, coloured cloths, foil sheets of silver, copper and gold and Thai perfume.

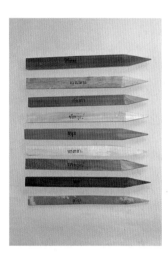

Above: Nine auspicious woods are placed in the *sao ek* hole, from above: *sak thong* (golden teak), *song badarn* (*Cassia surattensis*), *kankrao* (*Fragraea fragrans*), *chaiyapruek* (*Cassia javanica*), *khanun* (*Artocarpus heterophylla*), *thong larng* (*Erythrina orientalis*), *rajapruek* (*Cassia fistula*), *payung* (*Dalbergia*), *phai sisook* (*Bambusa flexuosa*).

Auspicious materials

The wood used to build the house can also bring misfortune. It is important to inspect for dead knots on the house posts. Undesirable dead knots on the post are those at eye level, those at the level where the fowls can peck at them, knots about one *sork* above the ground and knots below the position on the post where a beam is to be placed. Certain types of dead knots known as *rak-raek* or *chang om pleung* are forbidden.

House dimensions

The house dimensions can also be auspicious or inauspicious and are based on various calculations. The intended number of *khue* (roof crossbeams) is multiplied by 25 inches, as is the length of the *dunk* (plinth post). These two amounts are added together, then 11 is added, the total is multiplied by three and divided by eight. A sum which results in a remainder of five, means the dimensions are auspicious and will bring good fortune to the occupants. The appropriate height of the house posts is calculated on the same principle.

The width of the front door at the top of the stairway should be four times the length of the owner's foot; any wider and the occupants will suffer poor health. All other doors should be three foot lengths wide (any wider and fire will result).

Raising the house posts

In raising the house posts, the direction in which the post is laid on the ground is important. In the 4th, 5th and 6th lunar months when the *naga* (giant serpent) turns its head toward the west, the foot of the post should point towards the northwest. In the 7th, 8th, and 9th lunar months when the *naga* turns its head toward the north, the foot of the post should point to the northeast. In the 10th, 11th, and 12th lunar months when the *naga* turns its head toward the east, the foot of the post should point to the southeast.

In the 1st, 2nd, and 3rd lunar months when the *naga* turns its heads toward the south, the foot of the post should point to the southwest. In Suphan Buri, there is an additional belief that the house posts should not be raised in such a way that the posts will obscure their own shadows, which means that the proper time of the day has to be taken into account too.

Dimension of the house posts

The circumference of the base of a post foot is used as a unit of measure to determine the appropriate mortise positions (for the *rawd* and *tao*). The circumference is counted as one unit. The length of the post from top to bottom is then divided by this unit. Certain segments which signify bad omens should not be pierced.

The *berk na prom* ritual

The master builders of Thai houses in most areas conscientiously perform the *berk na prom* ritual involving the slitting of the gable top. The act of slitting and inserting the gable panel in position is preceded by the recitation of a special chant that each builder has learned from his mentor. Interestingly this ceremony is performed for the benefit of the carpenters and not for the house occupants.

Khue and the house owner

Before the construction of a house for newlyweds, a specialist is asked to examine the birth dates of the bride and groom to determine which remainders when doing the calculation are auspicious, usually odd numbers such as 1, 3, 5, 7, or 9. This auspicious remainder is added to the predetermined width of the *khue*. Thus if the width of the *khue* has to be seven *sork*, one *kueb* and a remainder of inches, the couple's auspicious remainder is added to make the required length.

The dimension of the cross-section wall panels

The width of this panel must not equal its length and various auspicious calculations are given. Thus if the *khue* is six *sork* wide, the wall should be five *sork*, one *kueb*, and six inches high. When the *khue* is seven *sork* wide, the wall should be *six* sork, *one kueb*, and five inches high. If the width of the *khue* equals the height of the wall, the house is sinister and uninhabitable.

Ceremony for the *chao thi* (land guardian spirit)

It is necessary to organize a ceremony in which offerings are presented to the spirit in return for permission to

---

The significance of the various post segments

The first segment is called *khun klang* and is considered a good omen.
The second segment is called *bang panaek* and is considered a bad omen.
The third segment is called *baek rawd* and is considered a good omen.
The fourth segment is called *thod salak* and is considered a bad omen.
The fifth segment is called *rak pang poei* and is considered a good omen.
The sixth segment is called *poei tawarn* and is considered a bad omen.
The seventh segment is called *plarn sat-tru* and is considered a good omen.
The eighth segment is called *kuha sawan* and is considered a good omen.
The ninth segment is called *khan sanied* and is considered a good omen.
The tenth segment is called *sied phraphum* and is considered a bad omen.

The relationship between time and house construction

Time	Consequences
The 5th lunar month	Brings great sorrow and sickness.
The 6th lunar month	Brings great success and wealth.
The 7th lunar month	Brings bad luck and loss of property.
The 8th lunar month	Brings theft and loss of wealth.
The 9th lunar month	Brings fame and prosperity.
The 10th lunar month	Brings lawsuits and misfortune.
The 11th lunar month	Brings deception, failure and death from sickness.
The 12th lunar month	Brings wealth, prosperity and attendants.
The 1st lunar month	Brings success and attendants.
The 2nd lunar month	Brings prosperity and protection from the enemy.
The 3rd lunar month	Brings fire and conflict with relatives.

The various stages in the ceremony for the installation of the first house post – the *sao ek*.

1. Monks chant prayers at the beginning of the ceremony.

2. The chief monk anoints the post with auspicious water using a lotus bud.

3. The owner prays by the *sao ek*. Note the banana tree tied to the top of the post.

4. The owner ties the red, yellow and green cloths around the *sao ek*.

5. Offerings are made to the spirits of the place.

6-7. The owner and friends help raise the post.

8. The *sao ek* is in position. Now the other posts will follow.

The *tri-nisinghhae yantra* cloth with cabalistic diagrams is tied to the *sao ek* in order to ward off evil spirits.

The old couple, representing the spirits of the place, sit inside this large wooden spirit house on the banks of a Bangkok *klong*. Coloured cloths are draped over the corrugated iron roof, while small pots will hold flowers on special occasions.

build a house on the site. These include betel nut, betel leaves, young coconut, red and white sweets made from rice flour and sugar, bananas, boiled eggs and pork. They are placed in the bottom of the holes for the bedroom posts. The specialist anoints the tops of the *sao ek* (main post) and the *sao tho* (second post) with holy water. The posts are decorated with pressed gold leaf, red and white cloths as well as cloths bearing sacred writings to ward off the evil spirits.

Prior to the erection of the the *sao ek*, offerings of a pig's head, *baisi* (a banana leaf decoration with flowers and topped with a boiled egg), a duck, a chicken, and red and white sweets are presented to the spirit of the land. A small banana shoot with three leaves, a stalk of sugarcane and pieces of red, green and yellow or blue cloth are tied to the top of the post. Offerings to the post consist of four *krathong* (a receptacle made of banana leaves) of cooked rice, seven candles and a *baisi*. After a brief ceremony the first post is planted into the hole. It must be planted straight and is allowed to lean to the east only. The size of each room is determined by the number of post-spans. For example, the normal size of a *ruen norn* is three post-spans.

Beliefs relating to the stairway

Odd numbers of steps are believed to bring good fortune. In addition, it is important that the stairway does not face west, as that is believed to be the direction of *bandai phi*, a stairway for the dead.

Digging the first hole

Diggers of the first hole for the *sao ek* should have the following names: In, Prom, Chai and Keo. If such-named persons cannot be found, the diggers are temporarily given these names for the duration of the ceremony. The remaining holes can be dug by someone with any name. The handles of the spades used in digging should be made from *rajapruek* (*Cassia fistula*) and *inthanin* (*Lagerstroemia*) wood.

Present-day beliefs

Although today the erection of the *sao ek* has largely been replaced with foundation stone laying, the tradition of placing auspicious substances in the hole is still observed. Small 30 cm woods from the following trees are placed in the hole:

1. *Sak thong* (golden teak *Tectona grandis*)
2. *Song badarn* (*Cassia surattensis*)
3. *Kankrao* (*Fragraea fragrans*)
4. *Chaiyapruek* or laburnum (*Cassia javanica*)
5. *Khanun* or jackfruit (*Artocarpus heterophylla*)
6. *Thong larng* or coral tree (*Erythrina orientalis*)
7. *Rajapruek* or golden shower (*Cassia fistula*)
8. *Payung* (*Dalbergia*)
9. *Phai Sisook* (*Bambusa flexuosa*)

Other objects included in the ceremony are: 12.5 cm sheets of gold, silver and copper, three bricks covered with gold-leaf, silver-leaf and a copper-leaf, nine

Above left: A water jar is frequently provided so that the inhabitants or visitors can wash their feet before ascending the steps to the house. This ancient tradition continues to this day.

Right: The various traditional Thai houses which make up the Jim Thompson museum are beautiful examples of this adaptable architecture. The underneath of the houses, traditionally left open, have here been adapted for modern purposes.

Opposite: The houses within the Jim Thompson compound are surrounded by fully-grown trees which provide a shady retreat from the dust and noise of Bangkok.

Right: Plai Noen Palace is surrounded by plants and trees.

semi-precious stones, nine scented incense sticks, a bottle of Thai scented water, a stone tablet inscribed with the auspicious time and date of the ceremony, and scented powder. At the appointed time a monk or layman invited to preside over the ceremony will drive the stakes into the bottom of the hole, sprinkle them with scented water and place all the above objects into the hole. Nine types of appropriate flowers for the ceremony are:

1. *Baan mai ru roey* (amaranth)
2. *Dao-rueng* (marigold)
3. *Rak* (*Calotropis gigantea*)
4. *Rajawadi* (*Buddleia paniculata*)
5. *Mali* (jasmine)
6. *Chaiyapruek* (*Cassia javanica*)
7. *Rajapruek* (*Cassia fistula*)
8. *Phuttaraksa* (*Canna indica*)
9. *Thammaraksa* (Heliconia)

Tree planting within the house compound

Certain trees are recommended for planting in the house compound and specific quadrants for their planting are also specified. To the east of the house, bamboo, *kum* (*Crataeva*) and coconut trees are recommended as these will bring happiness and good health. To the northeast, the planting of *yor* (*Morinda citrifolia*) and *saraphi* (*Mammea siamensis*) are recommended as these will ward off misfortune. To the south one should plant mango, *maplab* or persimmon (*Diospyros lotus*), and *maprang* (*Bouea burmanica*) as not only are the fruits

delicious but such trees will bring wealth. In the south-west, can be planted *chaiyapruek*, *rajapruek*, *sadaow* (*Azadirachta indica*), jackfruit, and *pikun* (*Mimusops elengi*) which as in the northeast section are chosen for their ability to ward off misfortune. Similarly in the west, tamarind, *mayom* (*Phyllanthus acidus*) and *putsa* (*Zizyphus jujuba*) are recommended to ward off ill-intentioned people and evil spirits. To the northwest of the house, *magrud* (*Citrus hystrix*) used in *tom yum* soup, lime, *sompoi* (*Acacia concinna*), and *ma-ngua* (*Citrus medica*) trees should be planted. Finally, in the north section, *putsa* (*Zizyphus jujuba*) and a variety of sedges, hemp and herbs are recommended to ward off black magic. Certain texts also recommend *matoom* (*Aegle marmelos*).

Trees forbidden in the house compound

There are restrictions against the following trees and plants in a house compound: *pho* (*Ficus religiosa*), *sai* (banyan tree), *samrong* (*Sterculia foetida*), *takien* (*Hopea odorata*), *krathum* (*Anthocephalus cadamba*), *lantom* (*Plumeria*), *salatdai* (*Euphorbia antiquorum*), *tao rang* (*Caryota*), *maroom* (*Moringa oleifera*), *rak-rae* (dahlia), *makok* (*Spondias pinnata*), wild *nang yam* (*Clerodendron*), *chuan-chom* (*Adenium coetaneum*), pine tree, camachile tree, *chaba* (*Hibiscus rosasinensis*), *puttarn* (*Hibiscus mutabilis*), the bottle gourd, and *mafeung* (*Averrhoa carambola*). Nowadays, taboos against certain plants and trees are mostly ignored.

House Components

Over the centuries the components of traditional Thai houses have evolved into a complex set of posts, beams, boards and panels each with their specific function. Different woods are used for certain components. The first three components – *ngua*, *kongpat* and *rae* – form the foundation and are not visible.

Ngua. Four round lengths of *thong larng* (*Erythrina orientalis*) wood, 50-70 cm long and 15 cm in diameter, are placed horizontally at the base of each post. They transmit the gravitational forces from the *kongpat* to the ground. Their function is to prevent the building from sinking and they are the equivalent of a foundation stone in a modern building.

Kongpat. A 5 x 15 cm wooden plank, 50-70 cm long, is mortised through the house posts near the base. Sometimes a pair of *kongpat* are attached to a slot on each side of a post and are secured in place by a *samae*, a wooden nail (made of *Avicennia alba*) one Thai inch (2.083 cm) in diameter, driven through all members in a mortise and tenon joint. The *kongpat* transfers the weight of the post onto the *ngua*.

Rae or Ranae. A flat circular piece of wood, 5-7 cm thick and 30-40 cm in diameter, is placed in the bottom of the post-hole to transfer the weight from the post to the ground and prevent the post from sinking. It is generally made of *thong larng* wood. The *rae* or *kong-pat-ngua* combination functions as a foundation and either can be used. The *kongpat-ngua* is popular with houses in low-lying areas near watercourses because it can sustain more weight than the *rae*, but the latter is simpler to install.

Sao ruen (house post). A round post made of *teng* (*Shorea obtusa*), *rung* (*Shorea siamensis*), *makha* (*Afzelia xylocarpa*) or *daeng* wood with a diameter of 25 cm at the base and 20 cm at the top. The *sao ruen* is a very important structural member of the house, and therefore, has to be selected with the greatest care. Only hardwood posts of exceptional quality with dead knots in the right positions may be used. The height of any mortise bored into the *sao ruen* to receive the *rawd* and *tao* must be carefully calculated to ensure the owner's happiness (*see page 73*). The house posts are further classified into various different types:

1. *Sao ek*. The first house post to be erected at an appointed auspicious time and in a chosen location as specified by an astrologer.

2. *Sao tho*. The second house post erected to the right of the *sao ek* during the post-raising ceremony.

3. *Sao mor*. These supporting post for the *rawd* and *ra* rise to just under the floor, are slightly smaller than the main house posts and are more closely spaced.

4. *Sao nang rieng*. These posts support the extended eaves and are found at the sides of the house.

5. *Sao trii* or *sao phon*. These are the house posts

Opposite top: The foundation for the Thai house is created by the use of *ngua* and *kongpat* which brace the post and stop it sinking into the ground. Sometimes *rae* are used instead of *kongpat-ngua* as they are simpler to install. However in marshy ground the *kongpat-ngua* is more effective.

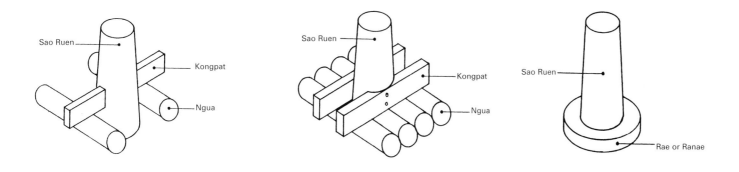

Sao Ruen
Kongpat
Ngua

Sao Ruen
Kongpat
Ngua

Sao Ruen
Rae or Ranae

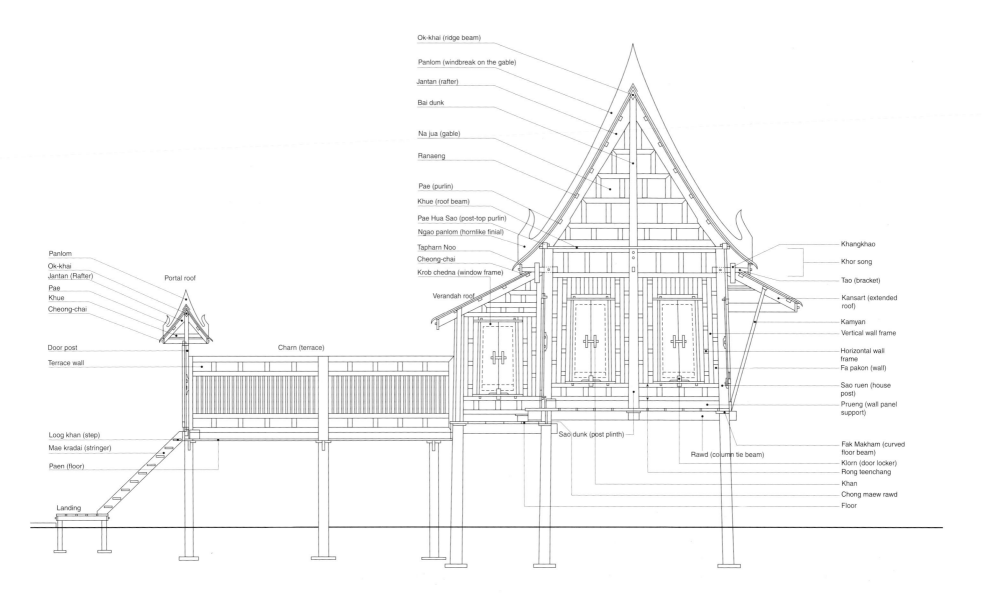

Ok-khai (ridge beam)
Panlom (windbreak on the gable)
Jantan (rafter)
Bai dunk
Na jua (gable)
Ranaeng
Pae (purlin)
Khue (roof beam)
Pae Hua Sao (post-top purlin)
Ngao panlom (hornlike finial)
Tapharn Noo
Cheong-chai
Krob chedna (window frame)

Verandah roof

Panlom
Ok-khai
Jantan (Rafter)
Pae
Khue
Cheong-chai

Portal roof

Door post
Terrace wall

Charn (terrace)

Loog khan (step)
Mae kradai (stringer)
Paen (floor)

Landing

Sao dunk (post plinth)

Rawd (column tie beam)

Khangkhao
Khor song
Tao (bracket)
Kansart (extended roof)
Kamyan
Vertical wall frame
Horizontal wall frame
Fa pakon (wall)
Sao ruen (house post)
Prueng (wall panel support)
Fak Makham (curved floor beam)
Klorn (door locker)
Rong teenchang
Khan
Chong maew rawd
Floor

Far left: The interior of Plai Noen palace. The upper part of the wall is decorated with designs for monks' fans by HRH Prince Narisara Nuwattiwongse, the palace's owner, while the lower part shows actual fans designed by the prince. The inner wall has three paintings of scenes from the Buddha's life enlarged from designs by the prince.

Left: The terrace area at Dr. Lek's house has been turned into a place to house a large Buddha image. The rear wall is in *fa samruad* style.

erected after the *sao ek* and *sao tho*, moving in a clockwise direction.

6. *Sao tor mor*. These supporting posts, the same height as the floor level, are planted directly in the ground to support the floor structure.

Rawd (post tie-beam). A 5 x 20-25 cm hardwood beam supporting the floorboards. It is mortised through a post with either end extending about 20-25 cm on each side.

Ra (floor beam). A 5 x 20-25 cm hardwood board is suspended under the *prueng*. Like the *rawd*, the *ra* is necessary to give additional support to prevent the floorboards from sagging.

Tong. A 4 x 5 cm (on the cross section) hardwood board placed between two *rawd* at 30-40 cm intervals to provide additional support for a special type of floor. When long planks are not available for floorboards shorter planks placed across the width of the house are used as substitutes. *Tong* can be used in lieu of *ra*.

Prueng (wall panel support frame). A teakwood frame made using 5 x 20 cm thick planks is attached to the house posts at floor level, holding the floor in place and supporting the walls on all sides. The *preung*, attached to the posts with Chinese-style nails, rests on top of the *rawd* and transfers the weight from the *ra*.

Phuen (floor). The floor of a traditional Thai house is made of 5 x 40-50 cm teak boards laid on the *tong* or *rawd*. They are joined by one cm diameter wooden dowels at 1.00-2.00 metre intervals. Sometimes *lin krabue*, flat 1 x 1.25 cm wedges made of *samae* wood, are substituted for dowels. Terrace floorboards are widely spaced with one-cm gaps for rainwater drainage in order to prevent the floor from rotting.

Fak makham (curved floor beam). This is a multi-purpose piece of curved timber (3.5 x 3.5 x 15 cm) so called because of its tamarind pod shape. It is nailed to the posts to provide extra support if there is a gap between the floorboards and the posts.

Fa (wall). The word *fa* refers to a variety of wall coverings made of panels of timber, palm leaves or bamboo fastened to hardwood or bamboo frames. They enclose the interior space of the house and partition it into different sections. Wall panels on the front elevation of the house are called *fa ud naklong* or *fa humklong* (cross panel) while partitions between the bedroom and the open hall are called *fa prajan hong* (room panels). There are many types of wall panels, but the main ones are *fa pakon* (wooden panels), *fa loog fak* (wood panels with a raised centre), *fa loog fag kradarn jiad*, *fa sai bua* (slatted wooden panels), *fa samruad* (with woven split bamboo), *fa khat thae* (bamboo panels) and *fa kradarn riab* (simple wooden boards).

Above: A traditional house with *fa samruad* panels.

Above left: Central region wall panels of the *loog fak* style.

Above right: A wall panel in the *khat thae* style.

Kansart (extended roof). This is a low-hanging roof projecting on all sides of the house at a lower level and with a less inclined slope than the main roof. It provides further protection from the tropical sun and rain. The *kansart* consists of *jantan kansart* (the rafter), *baeng klon* (eave divider) and roofing materials. The rafter is joined to a *tao* with a wooden nail (*khangkhao*) at the inner end while the outside is supported by a *kamyan* (truss) or a *sao nang rieng* post.

Tao (bracket). This is a 5 x 10 x 70 cm timber mortised through a post at 50-60 cm below the post-top and extending outward to support the *cheong-chai*, the roof, and the *jantan kansart*. The two types of *tao* comprise the *tao rhum* (twin *tao*) on each of the corner posts or the *tao rai* (single bracket) on the other posts. The bracket is larger at its base so that it can be inserted through the mortised slot at the top and pulled up until its base fits into the slot at a right angle.

Salak-duey (lock and pin). This is a 1.50 x 2.50 x 30 cm wooden wedge inserted into matching holes in the base of the *tao* and *jantan kansart* to lock them together. A 2 x 10-12 cm wooden pin is inserted into the extended *salak* (lock) above the *tao*.

Khangkhao. This is an 8 x 10 cm rectangular timber with a hole in the middle large enough to accommodate both a *jantan kansart* and a *tao*. A 2 x 15 cm wooden pin is used to hold both of these in place. The *khangkhao* functions similarly to the *salak-duey*.

Hua thian. A round tenon on top of a house post, 10-11 cm (five Thai inches) long and 4 cm in diameter, is used to hold the end of a *khue* to the head of the post and fits into a matching slot at each end of the beam.

Khue (roof beam). A 5 x 20 cm teakwood roof crossbeam is used to join the two posts, which are being pushed out by the weight of the *jantan*. This weight is transferred from the post to the *khue*. There are two types of *khue*, that in the middle of the room and those next to the *fa humklong* on both gabled ends of the house. The former is as large as the head of the post. The latter is larger, approximately 5 x 25 cm and is known as *khue ple*. It is angled on its outer upper end to support the *klorn peek nok* and is used to brace the upper section of *fa ud na klong* (the cross section wall panel) while the side walls are bracketed by *pae hua sao*.

Dunk. There are two types of *dunk*. The *dunk khwaen* is a flat timber 5 x 20 cm at the base and 5 x 12 cm at the top, fastened by wooden pins to the *ok-khai* (ridge beam) on one end and a *khue* on the other. The *sao dunk* is a long round pole, 20 cm in diameter, attached to the middle of a *rawd* by a *bark om rawd* (notched) joint.

Ok-khai (ridge beam). A long piece of diamond-shaped teak is placed at the top of the roof structure underneath the roof covering. It runs along the whole length of the house and extends beyond both ends of the gable top by 60-70 cm. The *ok-khai* is used to hold the gables, *dunk* and *jantan* in place.

Jantan (rafter). These 5 x 25 cm flat timbers are the main roof supports and make up the two sides of the triangles of the roof structure. The weight from the roof is transferred to the *klorn*, *pae* and *jantan* respectively.

Pae (purlin). There are two types of *pae*. The *pae hua sao* (post-top purlin) is a 10 x 10 cm beam running through the whole length of the roof structure and resting on top of the *khue*. Apart from transferring weight from the *klorn*, the *pae hua sao* also forms the upper section of the side panels of the house. The second type, the *pae larn*, are a 5 x 10 cm planks placed between the *jantan* and gable panels and parallel to the *ok-khai*. They transfer weight from the *klorn* to the *jantan*.

Klorn. These flat 1.50 x 7.50 cm lengths of wood are placed on top of the *pae* at 40 cm intervals. The first type is used for thatch roof covering and is smooth with a row of holes on one side for binding it to the thatch. It is secured to the *pae* with a *samae* wooden nails. The top end of the *klorn* is secured to the *ok-khai*

The roof structure of this pavilion has the *jantan*, *pae* and *klorn khor* in place.

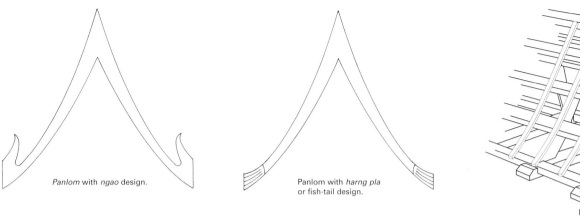

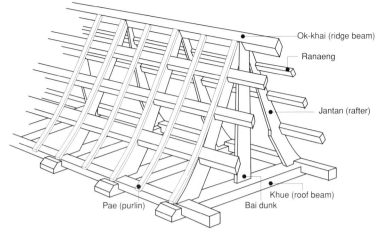

Panlom with *ngao* design.

Panlom with *harng pla* or fish-tail design.

Ok-khai (ridge beam)

Ranaeng

Jantan (rafter)

Khue (roof beam)

Bai dunk

Pae (purlin)

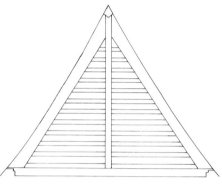

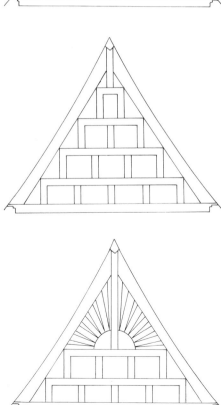

Above: The two most commonly found windbreaks, or *panlom*.

Above right: The various components of the roof structure.

Left: Some of the most popular forms of *na jua* are from top: *jua bai prue* (horizontal planks, *jua loog fak* (wooden panels similar to those on the walls) and *jua roob phra arthit* (with a sunburst pattern).

by a wooden pin while its bottom end is nailed to the *tapharn noo*. The second type for tiled roofs is called a *klorn khor*. The timber is serrated at 10-12 cm intervals to receive the *ranaeng*. It is nailed to the *pae* with Chinese-style nails.

Ranaeng. Lengths of 2.5 x 2.5 cm wood are placed lengthwise on top of the *klorn khor* and parallel to the *ok-khai* at 10-12 cm intervals in order to provide a fixing for the roof tiles and transfer the weight from the roof to the *klorn*. They are secured to the *klorn* by *samae* wood pins.

Cheong-chai. A 5 x 20 cm beam is attached to the end of the *tao* along the eaves. It supports the *tapharn noo* and carries the weight from the *klorn*.

Tapharn noo. A flat 1.50 x 1.75 cm length of wood is placed on top of the *cheong-chai* to brace the end of a *klorn* supporting the extending roof tiles so that the rainwater will not wet the *cheong-chai*.

Panlom (windbreak on the gable). A flat piece of wood, 2.50-3 cm thick, is attached to the end of the *pae hua sao*, *pae larn* and *ok-khai* to protect the gabled ends of the roof and roof coverings from the wind. The lower section of the *panlom* is decorated in *ngao* or *harng pla* (fish-tail) designs. *Panlom* are attached to the *pae* by nails driven from underneath.

Far left: A fish-tail *panlom.*

Left: The so-called *ngao* style panlom is sometimes described as a horned finial.

Below: A roof structure without any covering is put out to attract customers in front of a Thai house workshop along the road to Ayutthaya.

Below left: This unusual gable end from Suan Pakkad palace is carved with a five-tiered umbrella and palanquin and inlaid with glass mosaic.

Na jua (gable). Triangular wooden panels constructed in three different designs protect the gable ends of the roof structure from the wind, sun and rain.

1. *Jua loog fak* or *jua prommaphak*. The gable panel is constructed from many rectangles of wood in a horizontal and vertical design very much like the *fa pakon* wall design.

2. *Jua roob phra arthit*. This design of panel has a radiating sunburst design whose flat wooden slats are spread out with gaps between the sunrays for ventilation. This design is popular for kitchens.

3. *Jua bai prue*. The gable panel is made up of horizontally overlapping small flat planks. It is popular for the main house as well as the kitchen. When it is used above a kitchen the top section is usually left open for ventilation.

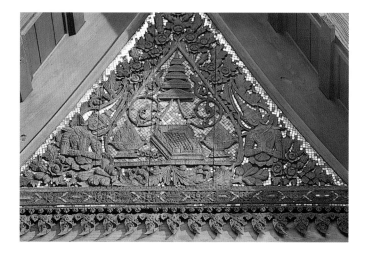

Langkha (roof covering). The roof covering can be made from a variety of materials:

1. Tiles. There are many types of terracotta roof tiles, usually named for their distinctive shapes, such as *krabueng harng mon* (round-ended tile) or *krabueng harng tat* (straight-end tiles). They are roughly 0.05-0.08 cm thick and come in pairs of male/female tiles.

2. Palm leaf thatch. This type of roof covering generally uses *jaak* (*Nipa fruticans*) palm leaves, easily found throughout the Central Region. The split palm fronds are reinforced at the spine edge with a 35 x 110 cm bamboo batten. The thatches are lashed to the roof structure in layers which overlap by about seven cm.

3. *Ya kha* grass thatch (*Imperata aundinacea*).This is tied to bamboo battens and layered on the roof.

4. *Faek* grass thatch (*Vertiveria*). The use of *faek* today is rare as it is hard to find.

All these roofing materials are available locally. Tile roofs absorb more heat than those of *jaak* or *faek*. Gaps at the the apex of the roof structure need a special tiled or thatched cover to prevent leaking.

Khaira (soffit). This is any part of the roof structure which extends from the walls or the gables, and is called after its location: the *khaira kansart* extends from the *kansart*, the *khaira na jua* from the gable.

Khor song. This is the upper section of the wall about one *sork* (50 cm) below the *pae hua sao* or *khue*. It is made in a rectangular *loog fak* design and runs above the main house panels on all sides of the house.

Rong teenchang. This lower wall section runs below the windows above the top of the *prueng*. Like the *khor song*, the *rong teenchang* is made in a rectangular *loog fak* design which runs all round the house. It is about one *kueb* and nine Thai inches wide (43.74 cm).

Chong maew rawd (literally 'a gap through which a cat can squeeze). This approximately 40 cm gap is between the bedroom and the *rabieng* (verandah) floors or between the verandah and the *charn* (terrace) levels. It provides ventilation from the ground to the main house; 1.50 x 7.50 cm struts placed at intervals prevent things from falling downstairs.

Pratu (house door). The width of the doors from the bedroom and kitchen to the verandah are usually three times the length of the house owner's foot. The door is wider at the base and tapers inward at the top as do the all the other uprights within the house structure. Its components comprise a doorframe, door panels and pins, a threshold and *darn khu* (twin bolt).

The main door onto the terrace. The width of this door is usually four times the length of the owner's foot. A small roof is added over the door frame to protect it from rain and create a visual emphasis.

Above: Different roof coverings: tile, *jaak* (palm leaf) and grass thatch.

Opposite: Differing styles of doors, some carved and inlaid with glass mosaic, others painted and yet others completely plain.

Window styles can differ greatly. Not only do they reflect the wealth and status of the house owner, but they also show the inventiveness of Thai craftsmen.

These unfinished wall panels with *loog fak* pattern are ready to be installed. They have been lent against the shed upside down as the carved *yong* should be under the window. They are a good illustration of the prefabricated modular nature of traditional Thai houses.

Nathang (windows). These openings are cut into the wall panels to provide light and air and are opened and closed with wooden panels. The components comprise:

1. *Krob chedna* (window frame). This is a flat 3-5 x 12.50 cm wooden rectangular grooved frame with mitred joints, whose base is wider than the top.

2. Window panel. Each window has two wooden panels some 3 cm thick. Each panel is secured to the frame at the top and the bottom by hinges made of 6 cm wooden pins 2.5-3 cm in diameter.

3. Window base. A 3-5 x 10 cm board runs below the window frame and extends by another 10 cm on either side. It is attached to the wall with Chinese-style nails or with *samae* wooden wedges.

4. *Yong*. This is a carved wood panel, 2 cm thick and 20-25 cm high, placed below the base of the window to provide decoration and visual emphasis.

5. *Ok-lao* (mullion). A hinged 3 x 5 cm timber upright is attached vertically to one window panel to cover the slight gap between the two panels when the window is closed.

6. *Darn diao* (single bolt). This is a 30 cm long piece of 3 x 5 cm wood fixed to the middle of the window panel. It slots into the wooden brackets which are attached to each panel.

7. *Kob*. This type of bolt secures the lower section of the window. It is a flat 1 x 5 x 10 cm piece of wood which fits into a slot at the base of the window (on the inside) after the panels are closed.

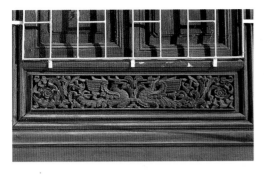

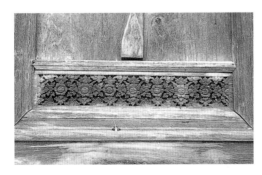

Above and left: The variety of the carvings found on the *yong* below the windows is quite remarkable. Some are geometric, others are floral, while several have animal motifs such as horses or chickens.

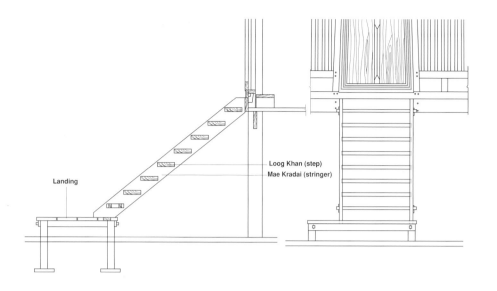

Left: A cross-section of a typical staircase.

Below: Traditionally, it is inauspicious to have an even number of steps and this one is no exception in having eleven.

Opposite: Often stairways have a small porch at the top to mark the entrance to the house.

Landing

Loog Khan (step)
Mae Kradai (stringer)

Kradai (stairway). The stairway of a traditional Thai house consists of the *loog khan* (steps) and the vertical components of *mae kradai* (stringer). In the old days, these stairways would not be permanently attached to the house. Made of wood or bamboo, they leant on the edge of the *prueng* and were drawn up onto the terrace at night to prevent access by predatory animals and thieves, being in effect a type of ladder.

Some had round steps and stringers, while others were rectangular in cross section. A round stairway consists of *loog khan* five cm in diameter and 10 cm diameter *mae kradai*. A square stairway consists of 3.5 x 7.5 cm *loog khan* and 5 x 10 cm planks for the *mae kradai*. The steps are mortised through the stringers at suitable intervals. In more developed communities the stairways become permanent and easier to use, being made of flat 3.5 x 20 cm planks for the *loog khan* and 5 x 20 cm planks for the *mae kradai*.

Today stairways can come in various shapes and sizes. They can be straight or have a dog leg, and some have a small porch at the top to mark the entrance to the house. Whatever their style, however, it is most important that the number of steps come to an uneven number. Staircases with an even number of steps are known as *kradai phi*, or stairway for the dead.

The Construction Process

1. The postholes are dug to the required depth of one *sork* 20 cm, one *sork* 22.5 cm or one *sork* 27.5 cm as specified by the master builder.

2. The ropes are secured around the *sao ek*.

3. The *prueng* has been removed from where it was roughly assembled to check the dimensions and the *sao ek* is ready to be raised using several ropes and many helpers.

4. The *sao ek* is raised to a vertical position.

The traditional Central Thai house is a magnificent modular structure in which many of the components can be prefabricated. They can be assembled on the chosen site relatively quickly, one house taking around three weeks. The posts and beams bear most of the weight of the roof, while the wall panels form a cladding.

The skill and craftsmanship seen in Central Thai wooden houses are considerable and, unlike the simpler *ruen krueng pook*, the owner would need to call in specialist builders and craftsmen. Nevertheless in the old days, the prefabricated components were erected using the labour of neighbours and friends under the supervision of a master builder.

After a period in the second half of the twentieth century when Thai houses were being pulled down many times faster than they were being built in favour of modern concrete houses and condominiums, today many people hanker after the traditional lifestyle associated with the Thai house, and, accordingly, in places such as Ayutthaya there is a thriving business in their construction with even some factories coming into being to produce all the necessary components.

5. The *sao ek* and *sao tho* are in position with a banana tree, sugar cane and coloured cloths tied around them. The other posts follow on being placed in a clockwise direction.

6. Once all the eight posts are in position they are secured with wooden braces.

7. After the posts are in position, work begins on the roof structure. Here the *jantan* and the *pae* are in place.

8. Next come the prefabricated gable ends which are lifted into position.

9. The prefabricated wooden *loog fak* wall panels are about to be lifted into position.

10. The long wall has three window openings coinciding with the three *hong* (post-spans) of the house.

11. The end wall panel is known as the *fa humklong*.

12. The *panlom* are being fixed in front of the gable end.

13. Once the walls, gable end and *panlom* are in position, the *ranaeng* battens are fitted to the *klorn khor*.

14. Here the structure of the *kansart* is being completed prior to tiling.

15. The terracotta tiles hook onto the *ranaeng*.

16. After the roof is completed the floor can then be laid without fear of the floor boards being damaged by rainfall.

Chapter 2
The North

Geographically, northern Thailand may be divided into two parts – the Lower North and the Upper North. Of the two, the latter is culturally more distinct. Whereas the Lower North has an architecture and culture similar to that of its Central region neighbour. The Upper North, on the other hand, which includes the nine provinces of Tak, Lampang, Lamphun, Phrae, Nan, Payao, Chiang Mai, Chiang Rai and Mae Hong Son, possesses a unique culture and architecture known as Lan Na.

Within the Lan Na cultural group, are several minority groups, such as the Shan (also known as the Tai Yai), found in Mae Hong Son, Chiang Mai, Chiang Rai, Lampang, and Tak, and the Tai Leu of Nan, Payao, Phrae, Chiang Rai and Chiang Mai.

Historical studies indicate that the earliest centre of Lan Na culture was the thirteenth century city of Yonok Chiang Saen, located in the northern part of present-day Chiang Rai. This city developed into a kingdom under Phaya Mengrai of Chiang Saen in the latter part of that century. This mainstream Lan Na culture, the culture of the Tai Yuan, or Khon Muang, spread from the early centres of Chiang Saen, Chiang Rai, and Chiang Mai to many communities in the area due to voluntary and forced migration occasioned by war over many centuries.

The Shan had settled in the present-day Mae Hong Son area long before it became a province of Thailand. Some were refugees from wars in the Shan States of Burma and others came with British timber companies or as traders. The Tai Leu are descendants of people who migrated from Chiang Rung in Sip Song Pan Na over the past few centuries. The area has also been settled by hilltribe minority groups but their vernacular architecture falls outside the scope of this book.

The Physical Setting

Previous page: A relatively new house in Phrae has been built using many traditional elements. It is a *kalae* house with modifications such as the greater use of fretwork detailing and the double porch, adaptations which have become increasingly popular.

Top: The Pai river valley lies between Mae Hong Son and Pai. Settlements originally occurred along river valleys such as this.

Above: A view towards the *chedi*s of Wat Lok Loli and Wat Chiang Yuen, Chiang Mai in the early morning mist.

The topography of Lan Na is a mixture of mountains, hills, valleys and plains. From the three major mountain ranges, the Daen Lao Mountains, the north and west Thanon Thongchai Mountains, and the Phi Pan Nam Mountains, flow the main rivers of the north and central regions, the Ping, the Wang, the Yom, the Nan, the Yuam, the Pai and the Kok, and it is these rivers which have been at the heart of the agrarian society of Lan Na.

As water is the most important factor for existence in an agricultural society, the selection of a site for permanent settlement is primarily based on the availability of a reliable water source and a fertile area suitable for planting, such as a river plain or valley. It was, therefore, in such places that the ancient Lan Na settlements were located. The geographical conditions also created a local agricultural technology: the *muang fai* or weir-and-channel irrigation systems, by which water from distant sources at higher elevations was brought to the lower-lying rice fields. An outstanding characteristic of these Lan Na villages and houses is that they were situated in an extensive area of greenery which created a shady and tranquil atmosphere.

The physical pattern of the Lan Na village, whether in a river plain, in a valley, or even on a hillside, is similar – a cluster of houses sub-divided into smaller groups. Each group consists of houses close together sharing a small yard. The village has a main thoroughfare with paths leading to the particular groups of

Above: This mural painting in the Viharn Lai Kham of Wat Phra Singh Voraviharn, Chiang Mai, shows the daily life, houses and dress of Lan Na people.

Far left and left: Other mural paintings from the same temple show that Lan Na women were usually bare breasted, while the men wore *chung kraben*, a piece of cloth wrapped around the waist and passed through the legs to make baggy trousers. Both men and women smoked cheroots. c. 1825.

Right: The house which formerly belonged to Chao Mae Yod Kham in Lampang is now owned by Kittisak Hengsadeekul. It is around 100 years old and being an excellent example of Lan Na domestic architecture has received a prize for restoration.

Below: A twin-gabled *ruen mai ching* with certain non-traditional features such as the use of the *phaya naga* (serpent) on the gable ends and stairway balustrade. (Wat Luang, Phrae)

Above: The village of Muang Pon and the temple in Mae Hong Son province. Muang Pon is the spiritual home of the Shan people. The *viharn* has a double-tiered high gabled roof.

Right: A spirit house for the *Chao Muang* (Lord of the Village) is constructed in the middle of every Shan village. This one in Muang Pon reflects the characteristics of Shan architecture in miniature.

Far right: The tail of a Shan-style banner shows their skill at handicrafts.

Left: A rice field hut on relatively tall posts. The 'bird wing' awning is thatched with dipterocarp leaves.

Below: The *viharn* at Wat Thon Kwain is a good example of a Lan Na temple in a rural setting. It was built in 1858 and has intricate carving on the gable ends and barge boards.

houses. It also has a square, an open area where the village pillar is enshrined. The fields of the villagers are in the same area. Surrounding the village, between the houses and the fields, is a community forest, the *pa phae* ('Goat Forest'), which serves as a fire and wind break and a place where villagers can gather forest products. At some point between the village and the community forest is the spirit house (*hor seua*), which is believed to protect people in the village from evil and keep them in peace and happiness. Beyond the community forest is the village's main planting area. In those villages where the fields are far away, shelters are built in the rice fields for those who need to stay over during certain phases in the rice growing cycle. Beyond the fields is the headwater forest (*pa ton nam*), which protects the source of the streams as well as wildlife. Traditionally, Lan Na communities were well aware of the importance of their headwater forests. They cut only what timber they needed for their houses, realising that maintaining the local ecological system was vital for the survival of the community.

In each village, apart from the houses, the village pillar, the spirit house, the fields, the community forest and the headwater forest, the other essential element of Lan Na culture is the monastery, or *wat*. The village monastery may be located in the centre of the village or it may be on high land within convenient walking distance. One monastery is frequently shared by more than one village.

Types of communities

Generally, a settlement begins with a house and grows into a group of houses with the development of transportation, trade, and exchange. As the community expands, its appearance and form change. Lan Na communities, be they Tai Yuan, Shan or Tai Leu, can be classified according to their size and importance, into three types.

Urban communities are large towns and important centres such as Chiang Mai with extensive links with other urban centres. Intermediate communities are midway between an urban and rural community and may be situated along main roads. Rural communities are small villages remote from an urban centre, where agriculture is the main occupation. This type of community has often preserved more of its local identity than those of the other two types and is thus a source of data about beliefs, religion, customs and traditional production.

Nevertheless, despite differences in scale, the three types share similar components including the community centre, the same types of public buildings which make up the community and the house. The centre of a typical urban community is a square, where the city pillar shrine is located. Nearby might stand the mansion of the governor, as well as an important monastery. There is also a large reservoir to store rainwater. Groups of buildings are located along the main road, and minor roads run from the main road to other building groups,

Above: A typical Lan Na style house belonging to the *kamnan* (head of the sub-district) in San Kampaeng district of Chiang Mai. On the right is a large rice granary. Note that the stairway of Lan Na houses is covered with a roof supported by two tall posts called *sao laeng ma*, which are believed to symbolise a dog standing guard over the occupants.

Left: This 60-year old Lan Na house in San Pa Tong is in single-gabled style. The *sao laeng ma* may be seen on the far right of the building.

some of these lanes curving with the topographical features of the area. Normally the village spirit house, which is believed to be the abode of ancestral spirits, is located at the edge the community. This shrine is a generally a wooden house supported by six posts built in the shade of a large tree and surrounded by a boundary fence. Offerings are made on a regular basis. In an urban community, apart from residential houses, there are houses, which have been adapted to serve as shops and buildings constructed as shops.

The layout of a rural community is generally similar but on a smaller scale. There is an open square in the centre where the village pillar is enshrined and where traditional ceremonies and public activities are held; there is a spirit house at the edge of the village and a small village monastery.

In order to appreciate Lan Na architecture the best sources are to be found in the monastery and the house. Typically, the house stands in its own yard. In the front, there is a spirit house and a shrine of the Four Guardians of the World. Near the house is a granary, pens and coops for animals, and storage sheds. Behind the house is a bathing area, a vegetable plot, and a shrine to the ancestral spirits. In the yard there will be one or more wells, depending on the owner's needs. Trees create an impression of coolness and tranquility. However, before discussing Lan Na houses in detail, we will look at the Lan Na temple which plays a central role in every day life.

Above: The Talad Chin road in Lampang has many wooden shop houses.

Left: A reconstruction of a typical Lan Na style grocery store has been created in Ban Fai restaurant in Phrae.

Northern Temples

Lan Na-style temples

Buddhist temples in Lan Na differ from those in Central Thailand in their size and proportions. The monasteries of both regions may be classified as being either town monasteries or rural monasteries, but Lan Na monasteries of either type are much smaller and simpler than their Central Region counterparts. In addition to the *ubosot* (assembly hall) and the *viharn* (preaching hall) that have walls, there are also open *viharn*, which are unique to Lan Na architecture.

The redented floor plan of the *ubosot* and *viharn* adds a gentleness to the form, and is echoed in the redented roof and its multiple layers. A fine example of a redented *viharn* with four walls of brick and mortar is Viharn Lai Kham in Wat Phra Singh in Chiang Mai. Another beautiful redented *viharn*, with wooden walls, is that of Wat Prasat, near Wat Phra Singh. Fine examples of open *viharn* are the Viharn Nam Taem at Wat Phra That Lampang Luang and the Viharn Chamadevi at Wat Pong Yang Kok, both in Ko Kha district.

The size and proportions of most Lan Na *ubosot* and *viharn* have a very human scale. Their architectural decoration, found on the corner pieces, the tops of posts, and the pediments, is mostly in beautifully carved wood. In urban monasteries, the carved wood may be gilded and decorated with glass mosaic in Lan Na style, while at rural monasteries, the carving depends on the skill of the artisans, and the designs generally differ from one locality to another.

Shan-style temples

Shan temples can also be divided into urban and rural temples. Most urban monasteries were built in memory of important people or on sites sacred to the community. The size, plan, architecture and decoration of a monastery reflects its importance. Rural temples have simpler architecture and are built of whatever materials are available in the locality.

The Viharn Lai Kham of Wat Phra Singh Voraviharn, Chiang Mai, was built in the reign of King Kawila in 1826. The roof has terracotta tiles. The *viharn* houses the Phra Buddha Sihing image.

Left: The Viharn Nam Taem in the compound of Wat Phra That Lampang Luang houses a bronze Buddha image cast in the reign of King Harn Srirat. The *viharn* was built in 1501 and is one of the most beautiful examples of Lan Na temple architecture.

Opposite: The main *viharn* and the *chedi* of Wat Phra That Lampang Luang. The main *viharn* was built in 1496. Inside there is a *ku* in *prasat* form. The *chedi* is plastered brick, clad with brass and copper. It was buit in Lan Na style during the reign of King Harn Srirat around 1766 in order to house a relic of the Buddha's hair.

The Hor Kham, which was the former residence of the governor of Lampang, has been reconstructed by Muang Boran in Samut Prakan province.

Below: The preaching hall of Wat Pa Fang, Lampang, houses a Burmese-style Buddha image. The columns are red and gold lacquer and the ceiling is gilded and embellished with glass mosaic stars.

Right: The *ubosot* of Wat Phra Non in Mae Hong Son has a Greek cross plan and is in Chiang Saen style. There are no windows and the building is surrounded by a spacious walled courtyard. The three-tiered roof is in *prasat* style and is surmounted by a gold umbrella.

The outstanding architectural characteristic of Shan temples is their multi-tiered roofs. Those with double surmounted roofs, each with a triple-layered roof are called *chettabun* and those with triple surmounted roofs, each with a four-layers of roofs are called *yon saek*. For very important edifices in which a presiding Buddha image is enshrined, the roof is of three, five, seven, or nine layers. Delicate roof decorations add to the grandeur of the architecture. Originally, the eaves, the pediments, and the roofs were decorated with wooden fretwork; more recently, a zinc-tin alloy has been used.

Monastery structures generally include the *ubosot*, the *chedi* (*stupa*), and the *viharn*, although some monasteries do not have an *ubosot* and, accordingly, the ordination of monks will not be possible there. The *viharn* can have many functions. Usually, it is used as a preaching hall, but it may also be partially partitioned to provide for a museum, living quarters for monks, or a Buddhist school. Most are rectangular in plan and are generally left open and screened off only in such areas where privacy and security are needed, such as museums or monks' living quarters. The floor is divided into different levels reflecting the varying functions, with the highest level (called *kha pan*), being reserved for the presiding Buddha image and being adorned with various decorative designs. The impressive painted columns in Shan *viharn* also serve to demarcate certain areas.

Above: The *viharn* of Wat Chom Sawan in Phrae was built in 1914 and is in Shan style. The tall red and gold columns have lotus petal capitals decorated with glass mosaic.

Left: The coloured paper stucture over the spot where the boundary ball was installed is in Shan style known as *jong*. Wat Hua Wiang, Mae Hong Son.

Far left: Inside the *ubosot* of Wat Hua Wiang, Mae Hong Son. The Buddha image known as Phra Chao Pala La Keng is a copy of one in Mandalay. The photograph was taken during a ceremony to install a boundary ball.

The Lan Na House

The Lan Na house, also known as the Tai Yuan, or Khon Muang, house, can be divided into two types. As we have seen in the Central region, this division is based on the physical appearance of the house and the materials: the *ruen mai ching* (the hardwood house, equivalent to the *ruen krueng sab* in the Central region) and the *ruen mai bua* (the bamboo house, or the *ruen krueng pook* in the Central region). The *ruen mai ching* house also has two types. The first is the well-known *kalae* house, belonging to the community's leading citizens. This type is distinguished by its fine craftsmanship and most noticeably by the *kalae*, which are elegantly carved wooden decorations at the gable top. For the most part, it is a twin house, the smallest type having one bedroom in each. There are two basic floor plans, which differ in the location of the staircase: in one, the staircase is parallel to and against the front of the house and is covered by the roof; in the other, the staircase is at right angles to the house platform. The more modest type of *ruen mai ching*, which may be either a single or twin house, has no *kalae*. These houses, owned by ordinary people which are influenced by the *kalae* house, the Panya- and Manila-style houses of Central Thailand and perhaps also by the *ruen mai bua*.

As in the Central region, the Tai Yuan house is raised high above the ground, with the space beneath the house serving as an open multi-purpose area. In the *ruen mai bua* and the *ruen mai ching* influenced by the *kalae* house, the staircase is covered by the eaves and leads up to the house platform (*charn*).

Adjacent to the platform is a multi-purpose, open porch-like area, called the *toen*, which has a wall on one side. The gable ends of the house face north and south and the sides east and west, the Tai Yuan believing it to be inauspicious for the gables to face east or west. Given the climate, a house in this region needs sunlight during the winter, and the general purpose *toen* is most useable if it faces south and the roof shelters it from the rain and sun. Another reason for the orientation of the house is religious. Monastery buildings such as *viharn* and *chedi* are laid down in an east-west direction, unlike those in Central Thailand, and it is believed that non-sacred buildings such as houses should not be oriented in the same direction as those that are sacred.

On the *toen*, there is a shelf, known as the *raan nam*, about 80 cm above the floor to hold the dippers and jars of drinking water with which guests are welcomed and members of the household refresh themselves. The reason the *toen* is called a multi-purpose area is that it is a place of relaxation for the family, a reception area for guests, the sleeping place for the father or sons and the place where the bodies of family members are laid out during funerals.

From the underside of the roof over the *toen* is hung a wooden frame, known as the *khwan*, for keeping water containers and other utensils. At the eastern

Above: The *raan nam* or water pavilion is a traditional feature of Northern Thai houses and holds the water jars for visitors. The house which is over 100 years old formerly belonged to Mae Kaew and is now owned by the Bangkok Bank.

Previous page: The *viharn* of Wat Chom Sawan in Phrae province. The entrance on the northern side has two porches with five-tiered roofs covering the double stairway. The *viharn* is in typical Shan style.

Left: Two examples of *raan nam* on the verandah of Lan Na houses. These shelves hold the earthenware jars and water dippers used to welcome guests.

Below: The large *toen* of a *kalae* house which has now been turned into restaurant.

Right: This house which embodies the characteristics of Tai Leu architecture, has recently been restored and is in the care of the Cultural Centre of Chiang Mai University.

Below: This house in Shan style (known in Thai as Tai Yai) in Muang Pon, Mae Hong Son, is a twin-gabled house whose eaves come down to cover the kitchen. The roof is thatched with dipterocarp leaves.

Bottom: Mats and other items are often woven at home and then stored in the multi-purpose area under the house.

Above: Inside a modified Lan Na house belonging to Phraya Kongka Kuenpetch of Phrae. On the walls are photographs of revered people such as King Rama V and senior relatives.

Opposite: The Ui Kham house within the grounds of the Ban Fai restaurant in Phrae has several glass-fronted display cases standing in a row along the wall. These house porcelain, silverware, lacquer items and betel chewing trays. Pictures of the former governor of Phrae and his wife, Chao Piriya Thepwong and Chao Mae Bualai hang above the middle display case, while large lacquer offering trays with covers stand on the right-hand cupboard.

A bedroom in the house of the *kamnan* in San Kampaeng district, Chiang Mai, which has several windows and sliding louvred openings at the front. Above the bed is a high shelf (*keng pala*) with a Buddha image, candles and vases.

end of the *toen* is an altar which extends like a shelf from the house wall, and, seen from the outside, looks like a protruding box. Near the altar, many people hang a picture symbolizing the day of their birth (known as a *tua peng*) and relics of their birth so that they may pay homage to these as well as to the Buddha image. The Tai Yuan tradition of locating the *toen* on the south keeps this general purpose area warm even during the cold season.

Adjacent to the *toen* is the bedroom, which is a private area, enclosed by four walls to protect occupants from the cold and danger. All members of the family sleep in the same room, which extends the length of the house. The bedroom has two doors, one leading to the *toen* and the other to the kitchen, which in the *ruen mai bua* is attached and which in the *ruen mai ching* is separated from the main house. Above the door frame of the bedroom on the inside is a sacred carved wooden plaque, called a *hamyon*, which is believed to protect people from evil. The word 'ham' means testicles, while 'yon' is derived from *yantra* which means protection against evil spirits. Thus in combination the *hamyon* serves to protect against evil spirits and ensure the fertility and prosperity of the family. It is usually installed at the same time as the house is erected. People often place other images near this sacred wooden plaque, such as pictures symbolizing the day and the year of their birth and religious pictures, as well as pictures of His Majesty the King and the royal family. At the bedroom door there is a high threshold designating this as a private area of the house which no one but those close to the family may enter. The family sleeps on mats or mattresses, laid on the floor and are protected with mosquito nets. Sleeping places in the bedroom are allocated from the innermost to the outermost. The innermost part of the bedroom is reserved for the owners of the house. Then comes the place for the married daughters or sons, followed by the area for unmarried daughters. Sons sleep on the *toen*, and in some houses, the father and the sons sleep there while the mother and daughters sleep in the bedroom.

The walls running the length of the bedroom are inclined outward while those across the width are vertical. The space in the bedroom is used for two purposes: sleeping and storage. The storage space is at the sleepers' feet. A special characteristic of the Tai Yuan house is a long board, called the *pan tong*, between the sleeping quarters and the kitchen, which are adjacent. This extends the length of both areas and marks their boundary. The main function is to allow people to walk out of the bedroom without disturbing those who are still sleeping. This is found in houses of both wealthy and ordinary people.

Most *ruen mai bua* are single houses in which the kitchen is not separated from the main house. However, many houses in certain areas, such as at Doi Saket in Chiang Mai, instead of being ordinary twin houses,

Above: The kitchen in the house of the *kamnan* in Chiang Mai is in traditional Lan Na style, in which the cook sits on the floor to prepare the food, which is cooked using charcoal.

have an extension from the main house which is at a right angle, like a wing, and this is used as a kitchen. The eaves of the kitchen are extended so that they cover the working area down below, a design which is very practical. In the kitchen there is a shelf for jars of washing water (*maw nam sua*) and a separate staircase makes it easy to fetch water from the well behind the house. Most of the utensils in the Tai Yuan kitchen are similar to those of the Shan and Tai Leu. There is a box filled with clay, and on the clay is an earthenware charcoal-burning stove or three stones to support pots. Above this stove is a shelf for storing food, pots and pans and other utensils. The utensils in a kitchen of a wealthy family are made of lacquerware, which is a Lan Na speciality.

In the house yard, there is a granary (*long khao*), a large mortar for pounding rice, a barn for animals and wells, all of which are very important in everyday life. The granary of a Tai Yuan house may be a building separate from but quite near the main house, or it may be just a large basket for storing rice kept next to the house and protected by the extended eaves. Those that are separate buildings are usually situated in the front of the house facing east which is also the direction in which a sleeping person's head points and is considered auspicious. Granaries are also a visible means of demonstrating the wealth of a family, as the larger the granary the more rice fields the owner must have. Most granaries are raised, but not so high that a man

Above: Another method of ventilating the kitchen is to have a panel just below the eaves which is simply covered with criss-cross lathes.

Left: Inside a rice granary which has been transformed into a kitchen.

may walk erect underneath. The area under the granary is used for storage and for pig pens or chicken coops. The barn is used for keeping animals, storing hay and straw and farming implements. Often there is a large mortar for pounding rice.

Tai Yuan wells differ from those of the Shan and Tai Leu. Traditionally, the Tai Leu share common village wells, and the Shan have a well in each house. Tai Yuan have one to three wells within their compound. One is at the foot of the staircase and water from this well is used to wash one's feet before entering the house and to water the garden near the foot of the staircase, which is planted with scentless ornamentals, flowers and climbers and is a unique characteristic of the Tai Yuan house. The second and the third wells are near the bathing area and supply water for washing and watering the rest of the garden and fruit trees. The wells in a Tai Yuan house are made of rounded bricks protruding around 50 cm above ground. Once a year during the Songkran festival they are thoroughly cleaned.

All house compounds have a spirit house known as the *hor chao ti* which is a miniature building on a single post. The *hor phi bu ya* (house for the grandfather and grandmother spirits) are only found in houses which can trace their lineages. A shelf for these ancestors is also installed in the bedroom and those from a different lineage may not enter. Every year in February and June a ceremony is held to feast the *phi bu ya*.

Two different types of Lan Na house showing how the staircase can be positioned. Both have tall *sao laeng ma*, the posts supporting the projecting roof.

The materials of the two types of Tai Yuan house are different. The *ruen mai bua* is roofed with large leaves, and the walls of the house are made of panels of woven bamboo strips or of leaves in a frame of woven bamboo. The floor is made of bamboo stems split open and flattened to make boards. The frame may be either hardwood or bamboo, or both. The roof of the *ruen mai ching* uses terracotta tiles and the walls and floor use hardwood boards.

A *kalae* decoration at the gable top is not found in the *ruen mai bua* and the ordinary citizen's *ruen mai ching*. It is only found on twin houses made of hardwood. In the case of the *ruen mai bua* the construction leads generally to a single house which is not strong enough for a *kalae*. Even when a *reun mai bua* is transformed into a twin house it is not given a *kalae*.

The Tai Yuan house embodies many of the qualities Tai Yuan Lan Na culture – peace, fertility, freshness and hospitality of the place and people. The light brown tones of the natural construction materials blend harmoniously with the greens of the trees and plants and the many colours of their flowers. Unfortunately, nowadays such scenes are only found in rural areas. The towns too were once much the same, but have become full of concrete modern houses, commercial buildings and shopping centres.

Opposite: The interior of Ruen Chao Mae Yod Kham. Note the large floor boards and the fretwork panelling around the upper part of the walls. Various items of lacquerware are placed around the room.

Above: Another view up into the roof structure.

Left: The side walls of this rice granary, within the compound of Chao Mae Yod Kham house are lattice-work panels.

Wooden roof shingles are used throughout the Lan Na area. In the past there were many teak plantations in the various provinces and wood was plentiful and cheap, as well as being much harder wearing than grass, leaf or palm thatch.

Above: The side view of a *kalae* house. The wall panel is prefabricated as a single piece. There are only a few small windows in order to keep in the warmth.

Right: A small *kalae* house in Chom Thong district, Chiang Mai. The kitchen is at the side.

there engaged in various tasks while talking to suitors. The *toen*, has a partition extending half a metre or so from the bedroom wall. As well as giving the *toen* some protection from cold winds, it also allowed the young lady's parents a place to discreetly chaperone any courtship which was in progress.

As with the *ruen mai ching* (and, indeed, all other Thai traditional houses throughout the kingdom) the bedroom in the *kalae* house is forbidden to non-members of the family, and trespass in this area is a serious offense against the ancestor spirits who reside there. Above the door frame of the bedroom is the *hamyon*. The two principal pillars in the bedroom, the *sao ek* and the *sao nang*, are always paired; they symbolize the happiness, peace and balance of the family.

The kitchen of the *ruen kalae* can be separate from the bedroom, or be its smaller twin. The house containing the kitchen, like its larger twin, is divided into two parts: an open area (*toen*) and a kitchen, while in some houses, there is also a store room. In the kitchen, stands a large corrugated iron box with a bed of clay. Earthenware charcoal stoves or three stones to support pots are placed on the clay. On one side, a shelf is hung for storing pots and pans. Above the beams is another *khwan*, like that above the *toen*.

The area between the bedroom house and the kitchen house is called the *homrin*. Above, where the eaves of the two houses meet, is a trough for collecting rainwater. As this makes this area very low, the floor

Details of the *kalae*. The motif, which is believed to be derived from the horns of the water buffalo, has become so identified with the Northern style that it is even used as a symbolic device on modern buildings.

is also lowered by 20-30 cm to ensure that people can walk through without bumping their heads and without disturbing people in the bedroom.

The *ruen kalae* has a high gable roof and there is no ceiling, so maintenance and repair can be done from inside the house. A pair of bamboo poles (called *khua lan*) for this purpose are installed on either side of the *sao ek*. These also brace the roof structure.

The beams and posts that form the frame of the house are generally fastened by mortise and tenon joints rather than nails. Beams are joined to the centre of the post, and the tip of the post and the rafter are shaped to fit each other. The size of the members depends on the load they must bear. The roofing is wood shingles (*paen klet*) or terracotta tiles.

The floor structure differs from that found in other types of house in that the joists are usually laid along the length of the house rather than across its width, and, as a result, they are closer together than in other kinds of houses. The heights at which the beams are joined to the posts they span are adjusted to obtain the various levels of the floor in the different parts of the house.

The walls of the *ruen kalae* differ from those of the Central Thai house. The latter consists of pre-fabricated panels, each as large as the span between two posts. The *kalae* walls, on the other hand, are composed of just one large panel for each side. At the corners of the house, the panels running the length of the house

Above: Another view of Ruen Mae Kaew house, a *kalae* house whose roofs almost seem over-sized in relation to the house.

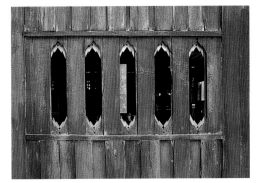

Left: Detail showing the sliding panel type of window in Muang Pon village, Mae Hong Son.

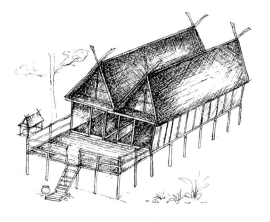

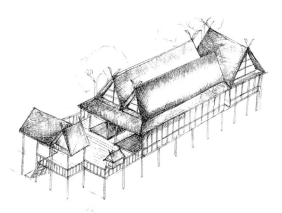

Left: The four different types of *kalae* house: 1) a small *kalae*; 2) a standard size *kalae*; 3) a large *kalae*; 4) a large *kalae* with modern features.

Above right: A rice granary in Sarapee district, Chiang Mai.

Opposite: The Phaya Jai *kalae* house, in Mae Yiea, Muang district, Chiang Mai, is almost 100 years old. This view shows the kitchen with its open bamboo walls. The many mature trees in the compound make it shady and pleasant.

extend beyond the ends of those covering the width; whereas, in the Central Thai house, the panels running the width of the house overlap the ends of those running the length. In addition, Northern wall panels do not slope inward.

The side walls of the *toen* have moveable louvre-like panels, called *fa lai*, to provide ventilation. These are 0.80-1.20 m high and consist of two panels with vertical slats set in the grooves of a frame. When slid one way, the spaces align and air can flow through; when slid the other way, the slats alternate with each other and the openings are closed.

The windows and doors open inward, with their frames on the outside. They are closed with a single panel, unlike in the Central Thai house, which always has pairs of panels.

The *kalae*, whose form is perhaps derived from buffalo horns, are boards attached to the gable ends of the roof to protect the tiles from being lifted by the wind. The ends are extended beyond the ridge of the roof and are beautifully carved so that they appear as though they are waving in the wind.

All Tai Yuan, or Lan Na, houses, no matter whether they are *ruen mai bua*, *ruen mai ching* or *ruen kalae*, are very similar. What distinguishes the *ruen kalae* is its greater refinement in terms of design and crafts-manship. In addition Lan Na houses may show slight stylistic differences from area to area depending on local taste and craftsmanship.

Right: Inside the house of the *kamnan* of San Kampaeng, Chiang Mai, are many tables with sacred objects. The *keng pala* (the cabinet decorated with white fretwork) are several Buddha images.

The Shan House

Opposite: A single-gabled Shan house in Muang Pon, Mae Hong Son. The roof is thatched with large dipterocarp leaves (*bai tong teng*). The walls of the house are woven mats and the smaller building is the kitchen.

Left: A mural painting of a low, single-gabled house which is typical of Shan roadside shops.

Below right: A single-gabled Shan house in Muang Pon.

The Shan house is often identified with the Lan Na house because they look similar. Both are wooden framed houses raised high off the ground with rather low eaves. However, the Shan house in the north of Thailand is in fact a significantly different from the *ruen mai ching* or *ruen kalae*, especially with regard to the roof, which has many levels and extended eaves on all sides.

The plan of the Shan homestead is of two types: a single house standing in a yard of 1,600-2,400 square metres enclosed by a fence, or a cluster of two or three, or perhaps four or five, houses in one yard. The former type belongs to a family of means who have been settled for two or three generations. The latter belongs to families that have settled more recently, when less land was available. There may be a large house shared by a big family or many houses. Some houses have separate granaries, while others have a granary at the rear of the house protected by the extended rear eaves. This type of granary is just a very large basket that can store enough rice for a family for a year. Some houses have as many as three such baskets. Each house has its own well.

Shan houses in urban and in rural communities can be divided into three types: the residential house, the shop house and the shop. The size and function of the residential house will vary according to the owner's needs and financial status. The two main architectural differences are the single- and double-gabled house.

The single-gabled house

This is a small wooden house with a single roof (3-4m x 6m). It is relatively narrow and elevated above the ground, but is not high enough for a person to walk underneath and the space is therefore not used as a work area. This type of house is built by a newly-settled family or as a temporary house. It has two rooms: the bedroom at the rear and the open *toen* at the front. adjacent to and in front of which is a small platform (*charn*). This is lower than the *toen* and serves as the

The *keng pala* or shelf for sacred objects within a Shan house. In front of a picture of a monk are many vases of flowers. Above is a cut paper decoration. At the left hang pictures of the Buddha. At bottom right may be seen a portrait of King Rama V with an offering tray in front.

landing of the staircase. The landing and the staircase are covered by the roof. The platform is extended along the side of the house, and this extension is enclosed and serves as the kitchen, covered by the extended roof. On the outer wall of the kitchen is a shelf protruding from the building, known as the *keng*, a feature unique to Shan houses, both large and small. Similarly, on one of the walls of the *toen*, there is another protruding shelf, the *keng pala*, which is used as an altar.

The frame of the house is made of hardwood, with wall panels made from woven strips of bamboo. The floors of the bedroom and *toen* are made of hardwood while those of the porch and kitchen are bamboo. The roof structure is also bamboo and the roof covering consists of large leaves.

The kitchen of a modest house may be simply a corrugated iron box or a wooden box lined with corrugated iron. This is filled with clay, and an earthenware stove or a tripod for the pots stands on the clay.

As with the Lan Na houses, the bedroom is the most private area and is enclosed, but not divided internally. Seen from the outside, it has one continuous wall, and there are few windows – maybe only four or five louvre-like ventilation openings (*fa lai*) – in order to keep the room as warm as possible in winter. The women of the household sleep in the bedroom, each in a mosquito net, while the men and any male visitors sleep in the *toen* area.

The double-gabled house

This large house is raised high above the ground and has two rooms, one under each gable. Generally, one serves as a bedroom and the other as a kitchen. The space beneath the house, which is about 2.20 metres high, is a multi-purpose area for rest, work and the storage of implements, carts and other vehicles, rice, firewood, and, in some houses, for keeping animals. The house is oriented so the sides face north and south. This is suited to the weather conditions in winter; the house receives enough sunlight to stay warm. The bedroom and the kitchen are always separate. The bedroom is held to be the principal part of the house and is larger than the kitchen, in accordance with the Shan belief that the two gables of the double-gabled house should not be the same size. Where the eaves of the two houses join, a gutter is installed to receive rainwater draining off the roofs. The floor underneath this gutter is lowered to give adequate headroom.

The floor plan of the double-gabled Shan house is similar to that of the Lan Na house. The main house has the bedroom in the rear and the *toen* in the front. The *toen* is once again a multi-purpose area used for receiving guests, dining, relaxing, as well as being the sleeping area for the men of the family. It is also used for merit-making ceremonies and laying out deceased family members during funerals. The smaller house is used as a kitchen and a storage space for agricultural products such as maize, rice, onions and garlic. The

Above: A Shan woman prepares the strips of large leaves for the roof covering.

Opposite: A Shan house in Muang Pon with double gable and an awning beneath (the so-called bird's wing eave) which covers the staircase.

storage area is fitted with rectangular frames with bamboo slats for hanging things. At the rear is the kitchen, which has a shelf for food, pots, and pans, and, in a corner, a stove box, like in the single-gabled house.

The walls of the kitchen are slatted bamboo for ventilation. The platform between the two houses joins the washing area at the rear and the front porch and a staircase, which is covered by the roof. In some houses, there is a bench on the platform, and a shelf holding a jar of drinking water for the guests. Between the *toen* and the platform is a low balustrade or a wall with louvre-like panels (*fa lai*).

One of the defining features of the Shan house is the protruding shelf in the *toen* area and sometimes there are similar shelves in other parts of the house.

Shop houses

Originally shops were simply ordinary houses selling a few goods. However, as commerce increased, some houses on main routes were modified to serve as shops below and houses above or alongside.

The shop house can be either a single- or double-gabled house. The additions for sales and storage are usually on one side thereby separating them from the front staircase and platform to preserve family privacy. If the street is on one side of the house, the roof can be extended to cover the shop, but if the street is at an end of the house, a separate single-gabled building only slightly raised above the ground is built next to the house. The structure and materials of the main house and the addition are the same: a wooden framework and roof structure, with a roof of large leaves. Some buildings are built primarily as shops. Rural shops are usually one-story row houses or the modified ground floors of single houses, in which the proprietors live above in the house part. The front is always left open. Urban shops are usually two-story wooden buildings having three 'rooms' (i.e. four posts across) each measuring 3.50-4.50 metres in width. The front forms the shop, and the rear a kitchen. On the upper floor are a store room and a bedroom, with a protruding balcony on the street side, which shades the shop entrance during the day.

The front of the shop is closed at night using a series of hinged panels, which open and close in accordion fashion. There are three rooms on the upper floor, with the middle room having a door onto the front balcony while the other two rooms have windows. The door and windows are flanked by slatted windows, giving the front of the building a distinctive appearance. The roof style has been influenced by the Central Thai house, but the details such as doors, windows, and the carving and design of balustrades show the inspiration of Shan architecture. Nowadays, good examples of Shan shops are rare, but some can be found in Mae Hong Son province. The framework of the building and its roof, floor, and walls are made of wood, while the roof is corrugated iron or tiles.

Above: A *teng na* with no raised platform and very low roofs. Such shacks are known as *tup nok kwaek*, so called from their resemblance to a particular species of bird.

Above right: This *teng na* has a wooden structure, no wall panels and a thatch of big leaves.

Below right: A Shan rice-field hut in Muang Pon of the *tup nok kwaek* style.

Field shacks (teng na)

In northern Thai villages, as elsewhere in the kingdom, the houses are usually grouped together in the same area while the fields are often located some distance away. People have to walk quite far to go back and forth between their home and the fields. During the planting and harvesting seasons, this is not convenient, so a field shack is essential. Looking across the rice fields, one can see many such field shacks which lend beauty to the fields. Villagers who live very far away from their fields and need to stay in them for long periods build more permanent field shacks.

Generally, field shacks are raised high off the ground and have no walls, but simply a low balustrade. The space underneath is used for storage, cooking and resting. The platform of the shack, accessed by a ladder, is sheltered by a gable roof. One or both of the gable ends of the shack may be sheltered by smaller curving, conical, or flat awnings, whose edges are supported by one to three posts. The main roof slopes down to cover the edges of the platform, so that when seen from the outside, only the roof and the open space beneath the shack are visible. The roof keeps the sun and rain off the platform, which is used for sleeping and storage. In some shacks, another platform is installed above the main platform for storage, while in others the eaves are extended almost to the ground and supported by additional posts, providing a large area for storing rice. Shacks which are more permanent, may have very

low roofs of the *tup nok kwaek* style, instead of the awnings, a modification particular to Lan Na. Though they can be built quickly and easily, field shacks can be used for a long time and their architecture has a simple and functional beauty.

Barns (seung)

Animals like cows and buffaloes used to be an essential part of a farmer's life, and after a long day's work, they need secure shelters. The barn is thus another important small-scale structure within the compound of a Thai house. Normally, barns are located near the house, within sight for safety. The architecture of these open buildings is simple: the posts may be simply rough tree trunks stripped of their bark standing on a tamped earth floor. The gabled roof with awnings most frequently has a bamboo framework with a thatch of large dipterocarp leaves.

Far left: The *rong krok* is where the rice is pounded in a large mortar to remove the husks. Like various other structures within the house compound it is a very simple open shed.

Left: This women standing in front of the rice granary, is dressed in typical Shan style.

Below left: A Shan-style pavilion built over a well.

The barns are also used to store implements, and the large mortar and pestles for husking and polishing rice may also be set up there.

Rice granaries (ye khao)

There are two kinds of rice granaries: one is separated from the main house, the other is attached. The latter is simply the space beneath the eaves, which are extended almost to touch the ground and supported by posts. The rice is stored in a large basket. Separate granaries are like small houses; they are elevated high off the ground with the ridge of the roof parallel to that of the house. In some, the rice is completely enclosed within wood framed walls, and stands on a hardwood floor capable of withstanding a significant amount of weight. The walls may be either hardwood or bamboo boards, with the wall studs on the exterior. Some granaries have low walls, with the rice being stored in a large basket. The space beneath the storage chamber may be used for keeping pigs and chickens or for storing farm implements.

Pavilions (sala)

In Thai villages, one can often see beautiful small pavilions of many different styles and sizes. Some are used simply for relaxation, while others have a specific function, such as protecting a well.

Traditional Beliefs

Nowadays less importance is given to beliefs relating to all aspects of Northern Thai houses, but in the past these were an important part of everyday life and various ceremonies and rituals were carried out at specific times of the year or on special occasions such as moving in to a new house, as well as ceremonies connected to the different rites of passage. Those carrying out such rituals were usually men who had been monks or were associated with the temple and were respected by the villagers. Such a person would be able to determine auspicious times and interpret omens.

There were also numerous taboos or omens known in the local language as *kud* – things or events that were inauspicious. These could arise as the result of human actions or from the presence of inauspicious animals or unnatural events. The force of such events could be neutralized by asking a monk to come and perform a *ton kud* (bad omen removing) ritual.

Various *kud* relate to the house, its construction and surroundings. The use of posts which have many marks, splits or knots oozing sap or gum are considered to be *kud*. A rice mortar which is damaged should not be repaired. The stairway of a house should not be enlarged, one should not use a new roof with old posts or an old roof with new posts. When building a new

Left: A Lan Na style house with a fretwork balustrade and prominent *sao laeng ma*.

house it should not be built higher than the Buddha image in the temple, nor in line with the image. A house should not be built over a river, a road, a cemetery, a deserted monastery or an old pond.

Many trees are considered to be *kud* and should not be allowed to remain standing within the compound. These include trees that are damaged, dead or have fallen down, those that have been struck by lightening or have an unusual shape.

Regarding the actual construction process, it is considered inauspicious to finish building both houses of a twin house at the same time, nor should the sizes of the two bedrooms be the same. The house should not be given additions nor be made smaller. Certain events which might occur during the construction process could also be inauspicious. Thus if during the erection of the house posts, the scaffolding and the post fall over, then that post should not be used, or if it has to be used then a ceremony to remove the *kud* must be performed.

There are also various proscriptions relating to the house compound. A house must not be enlarged or reduced in size while standing on the same piece of ground. Certain trees should not be planted near the house, including bamboo, *nam tao*, banana trees, *thong larng*, *pikul*, *champa* and *yor*. The practical reason behind this belief was that the flowers, leaves, sap and pollen from the trees could affect the health of the inhabitants or cause an allergic reaction.

As well as the *hor phi bu ya* in the house compound, a shelf for the ancestor spirits is erected within the bedroom. It is believed that they will protect their descendants from any danger.

The siting of the well and the road to the house should not be in line with the front gate or the entrance to the house. The gate should not be enlarged more than the width of the path. The granary or the rice pounder should not be moved 'across the house', namely from the east to the west and vice versa, or from the north to the south.

Although some of these beliefs persist they are not as influential as in the past. Unfortunately those relating to the prohibitions against the partial repair or enlargement of an existing house have resulted in virtually all the traditional *kalae* houses having to be pulled down when the owners needed more living space. Furthermore as deforestation has increased and there have been various laws clamping down on illegal logging, hardwoods have become increasingly hard to obtain and very expensive, making concrete or brick houses a more attractive proposition. Thus, however powerful such beliefs may have been in the past, they have not managed to prevent virtually all the old wooden houses from being taken down.

Building a new house, in the old days, would have involved a trip by the owner and his neighbours into the forest to chose suitable trees for the house posts. If during the cutting down of the tree, it were to fall across another it would be considered unsuitable for house construction and would be abandoned. In addition, the direction in which the tree fell could also be used to make various predictions.

As with much of Thai life, whether in the north or elsewhere, auspicious times must be chosen to begin construction. These will usually be determined by a monk or an elder associated with the monastery. In the past, times were also chosen for going to the forest and digging the post holes. Apart from choosing an appropriate month, the times must not coincide with an inauspicious day. The phases of the moon must also be taken into consideration and the birthday of the house owner. As can be imagined the calculation of these complex temporal interactions requires a good knowledge of traditional texts relating to such matters.

Choosing an auspicious location involves closing one's eyes, reciting a request for a favourable location and choosing between different bags. A bag of soil indicates that the owner's endeavours will be successful; a bag of bark chips means an unhealthy location; a bag of egg shells will not bring prosperity; a bag of flowers will ensure fame and position in society.

The complex traditional procedures for building a Northern house are usually neglected nowadays, especially in urban areas. However, such practices are still observed in remote spots where people adhere to conventional ways of life and cultural norms. The traditional procedures for the construction of a Lan Na house have been compiled from documents and interviews with local scholars. Although some of these procedures and rituals are no longer performed they are an important record of Lan Na culture.

Building a Northern Thai House

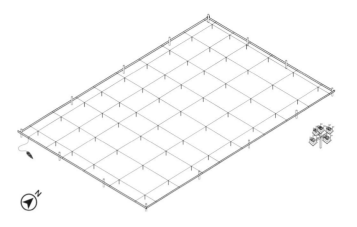

Preparing the site

Once the auspicious times for the various stages of house building calculated, the construction site is measured and the perimeter of the house marked out with wooden stakes. These are driven into the ground and secured with ropes made from nine strands of cotton string to make a grid for the positioning of the house posts. Another method for positioning the house posts is to use a measuring stick, after the grid has been created, to determine the width and length of each room as desired by the owner of the house. In the past, this type of measurement was done with ropes made from specific auspicious materials of particular colours. Once the house perimeter has been determined, the floor beams (*khue*) and purlins (*pae*) are placed together so that the holes for the post tenons at the end of each timber are matched. The beams are positioned across the width of the house while the purlins are positioned along the length. House posts are then placed at right angles to the beams and purlins. A house may face any direction the owner wishes but most houses tend to face north or south. Wooden stakes are driven into the ground through holes in the floor beams and purlins to mark the position of the actual holes to be dug for house posts.

Offerings to the four spirits and hole digging

According to traditional beliefs, the offering ceremony to the four spirits must be performed in the evening prior to digging the house post holes. The auspicious post (*sao ek*) is the second post from the partition wall on the eastern side of the house. The hole for this house post is dug first, followed by the hole for the secondary post (*sao tho* or *sao nang*), located opposite the *sao ek* on the western side of the house.

After the position and number of house posts is determined, the craftsmen will prepare the timber by cutting, holing, shaving and planing it to the desired length and size. The success of this construction stage is ensured by a *kroa tang khan* ritual, performed to pay respect to the builders' teachers, a ritual which may also be performed during the post raising stage.

Raising the posts: the sao ek and sao nang

On the day of the house post raising, the villagers will come to assist in carrying the *sao ek* and the *sao nang* posts to the holes. According to traditional belief, when the posts are laid on the ground their tapered ends must point in an auspicious direction, which is determined according to the particular day on which the house posts are raised. The soil from the holes must also be thrown in that direction. The larger ends of the posts are placed next to the holes, slightly raised above the ground and supported on a wooden block. The temple elder will tie a coconut shoot, a banana shoot and a sugar cane to the auspicious post. Other items used for this purpose mentioned in some ancient texts are a bunch of bananas or young coconuts, the

Top: Digging the post holes with that for the *sao ek* being in the middle of the series of posts.

Above: Lifting the *sao ek*. Once the necessary rituals have been carried out, the owner and the neighbours help in lifting the post into position.

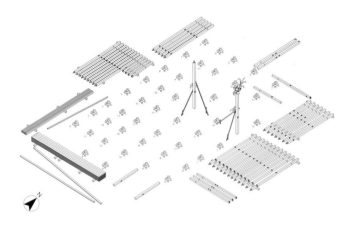

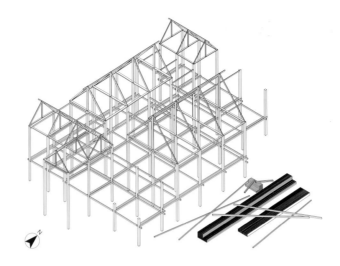

shirt of the male house owner and auspicious leaves for the particular day on which the ceremony is performed. After the ceremony, the leaves are placed at the bottom of each hole.

Today it is difficult to find the auspicious leaves specified in ancient texts because the forests are fast disappearing and the ritual of placing the leaves at the bottom of each post hole is usually omitted. In certain areas, a ceremony is held to ask the *phaya nak* (a mythical serpent), who is the landowner of the particular area, for permission to use the land.

In cases where the carpenters want to be certain about the correctness of the house structure they may assemble the beams, purlins, plinth and rafters together in a pre-test. Any disparity in the parts can be corrected before the actual construction. This pre-test is known as *dao harng* (or *thao rarng*). The carpenters may drive a pointed stake about one *sork* long through the holes in the beams and purlins into the ground. A measuring stick is used to determine the right angles among the parts by the use of equal diagonal lines. However, this has now been replaced by a T-square.

The other posts and tying the cabalistic cloth

After the *sao ek* and *sao nang* have been raised, the rest of the posts can be raised in any order. House posts come in a variety of shapes from round to square or octagonal. Round posts were mainly used until about 30 years ago when square posts became popular.

In some cases, square posts under the house are made of concrete for strength.

House post raising requires a number of labourers under the supervision of a *sala kao*, who is usually an expert in house building. Four men, with the help of supporting poles, are required to raise a post with a diameter not greater than 20 cm. With a 30 cm post, the men use prongs made from strong coconut trunks to support the tenon (*duey*) on top of the post, while another man supports the larger end of the post with his shoulder. Wooden planks are placed around the hole to brace the post until it is vertical. A piece of wood is then nailed to each raised post to provide the necessary temporary support.

When all the posts have been raised, the holes are filled with sand, believed to prevent weevils, and loose soil. The next step is to place a square white cloth with cabalistic writing on top of the post in order to ensure happiness and prosperity for the household. A hole is made in the middle of the cloth to allow the tenon to pass through. The sacred cloth is usually only placed on certain posts, such as those in the bedroom but not those in the kitchen or on the verandah. However, in certain instances, generally during a housewarming ceremony, every post receives a special cabalistic item. On such an occasion, a temple elder will attach either a bronze plaque, a sacred cloth or mulberry paper to the posts and the plinths.

Above: This series of drawings shows the stages in the construction of a classic, twin-gabled Lan Na house.

1. A frame is constructed on the site and strings are stretched to form a grid for the positioning of the post holes. This can be done once a ritual for the Guardians of the Four Directions has been performed.

2. The post holes are dug and the *sao ek* and *sao tho* posts are raised.

3. Once all the posts are raised and the frame for the floor is in place, the roof structure can be added.

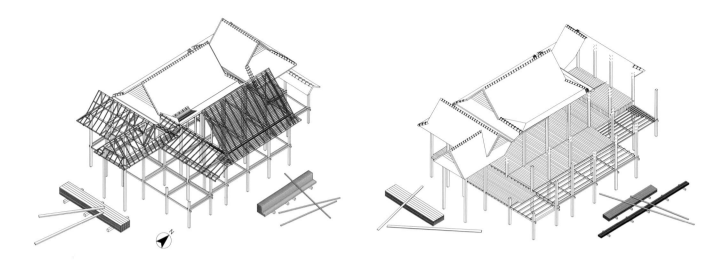

The roof beams, purlins and roof structure

The next step is the attachment of roof beams (*khue*) and purlins (*pae*), which are fixed to the width and length of the house structure respectively. For old houses (more than 40 years), each post has a tenon on which the beam is placed followed by purlins and the roof structure. Since the beams and purlins are the most important parts holding all the posts together, once they are successfully placed on the tenon there should be no problems with the rest of the structure.

For houses that are less than 40 years old a frame or *waeng keeb* is erected to hold the posts together and to facilitate the assembly of the roof beams, purlins and the roof structure.

When the posts, beams, and purlins are in position the next stage is the raising of the plinth (*dunk* or *sao dunk*), which is a piece of 5 x 10 cm timber placed in the middle of the beam along the height of the roof. The length of the *dunk* is usually half the length of the beam, sometimes with the addition of 15 extra cm. If a beam is 6 *sork* (3.30 metres) long, the plinth will be 2 *sork* (1.10 metres) or 3 *sork* (1.65 metres) long. There is a tenon not more than 3.5 cm long at both ends of the plinth. These are fitted to the holes in the middle of the roof beams and in the ridge pole (*ok-khai*), the topmost piece of wood in the roof structure. It is a 10 x 6 cm, diamond-shaped timber of the same length as the purlins. An appropriate hole is measured and drilled in the ridge pole to be fitted to the tenon on the plinth so that the end of the ridge pole will extend from the end of the rafter by 1 *sork*. The next step is to secure the rafters to the ridge pole and purlins. The rafters which are 10 x 6 cm timbers make two sides of the triangle for the roof to form a gable and support the *mai karp*.

The rest of the roof and the roofing materials

The *mai karp* are 8 x 4 cm timbers, the same length as the purlins, placed on top of the rafters. Both the rafters and *mai karp* are of the same width so as to provide smooth and secure bonding. They are fitted together with a *sae* (a wooden peg or wedge) or nail. The distance between the ridge pole and the purlins is dictated by the size of the room or by the length of the rafter. A room 3 metres square requires only one *mai karp* while a 4 x 5 metre room requires more than two. The *mai karp* are placed at equal intervals to distribute the weight of the roof structure evenly.

The next step is to place the *klorn* parallel to the rafters on top of the *karp* which are on top of the purlins. They are placed in pairs on top of the ridge pole, running through the *mai karp* and purlins and slanting down the eaves on both sides of the roof. The next step the *mai karn fa* (*ranaeng*) are attached to the top of the *klorn* at 10-13 cm intervals from the topmost section of the roof right down the eaves. The last step in the construction process is to cover the front pair of *klorn* with a *panlom* (windbreak).

This mural painting in Wat Buak Krok Luang, Chiang Mai, shows Chinese building a house.

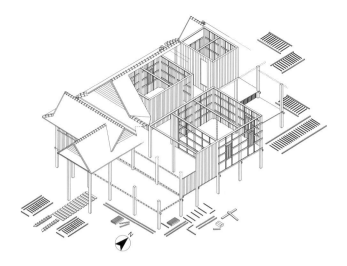

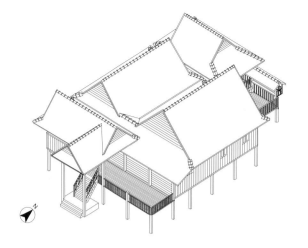

The *pan nam yoi* or *cheongchai* is a piece of wood used to support the roof structure and to increase the aesthetic appeal of the house.

Roofing materials are made locally and include terracotta tiles, pointed cement tiles, and curled tiles.

Floor beams, joists and floor boards

There are two types of floor beams, *waeng sord* and *waeng keeb*. The latter are more common in later houses because they are easy to assemble and are very strong. *Waeng sord* are found mostly in houses between 40-70 years old. The *waeng* act as beams to support the floor boards. The most popular size is 5 x 15 cm. They are inserted into the holes in the posts on the western and eastern sides of the house, running parallel to the roof beams. After a *waeng* is inserted into the holes a wooden wedge is fitted underneath to keep it level and attach it firmly to the posts. With *waeng keeb*, grooves are made on both sides of the post to support the *waeng keeb* at the same height as *waeng sord*.

After all the floor beams have been fitted, 8-10 x 5 cm timber joists are placed on top at right angles to the floor beams at approximately 0.30 metre intervals. They are placed parallel to the purlins to give support to the floor (*pae puen*). The floor boards vary in size ranging from between 15 x 2.5 cm to those which are 30 cm wide were used. Houses with thick posts, wide floor boards and large wall panels reflect the owner's economic status.

Wall joists, panels, door and window frames

Wall joists (*mai jen fa*) of 7.5 x 4 cm are placed in an upright position, extending from the floor to roof beams (*khue*) at 1 *sork* intervals, support the wall panels, doors and window frames. Exterior wall panels are attached first, followed by partition walls, which are usually attached horizontally to the wall joists, overlapping at the lower part. A space of approximately 1 *sork* (0.50 metres) is left between the walls and roof beams and purlins for ventilation.

Adding the ornamental and sacred features

After the partition walls have been attached, the remaining stages are the attachment of ornamental and other fixtures such as doors, windows, a shelf to accommodate the Buddha image, a water shelf, railings and *rarng charn*. The stringers of the staircase (*mae kradai*) and steps are made from 15 cm x 3.5 cm and 20 x 3.5 cm timbers respectively. The number of steps must be an odd number, such as 3, 5, 7, 9 or 11. Staircases normally face towards the east, southeast, or northeast.

The attachment of a special ornamental fixture known as the *hamyon* in a northern Thai house requires a special ceremony. It is usually installed at the same time as the new house. The length of the *hamyon* is equal to the width of the door which, in turn, is determined by a measurement derived from length of the owner's feet.

4. This stage sees the roof structure completed including the wooden shingles, which are the preferred roofing material for Northern houses.

5. The floor is completed.

6. All the staircases are installed, together with the verandah, the terrace, the altar for the Buddha image and the kitchen.

7. The last stage is the addition of the windows, the doors and other small details.

Chapter 3
The North-East

Isaan, as the north-eastern region of Thailand is generally known, is bordered by the People's Democratic Republic of Laos to the north and the east and by the Democratic Republic of Cambodia in the lower east. It covers an area almost one-third of the whole country – 170,218 square kilometres or 106.4 million *rai*. The region has 19 provinces: Loei, Udon Thani, Nong Bua Lam Phu, Nong Khai, Sakon Nakhon, Nakhon Phanom, Mukdahan, Ubon Ratchathani, Amnat Charoen, Yasothon, Roi-Et, Maha Sarakham, Kalasin, Khon Kaen, Chaiyaphum, Si Sa Ket, Surin, Burirum and Nakhon Ratchasima.

Geographically, the Isaan region is a plateau with two major river basins, the Sakon Nakhon and Khorat. The Phu Pharn Mountain Range extends through many provinces, from Ubon Ratchathani to Mukdahan, Nakhon Phanom, Amnat Charoen, Sakon Nakhon, Kalasin, Khon Kaen, Chaiyaphum and Udon Thani, to merge with the Petchaboon Range, which separates Isaan from the Central and lower Northern region, at Loei.

There are a number of major rivers in the Sakon Nakhon Basin: the Loei, Songkram, Yarm, Oon, Huai Luang, Ploo Harng, Kam and Huai Mook. The Hueng river defines the Thai-Lao border along part of Loei province, while the Mekong river forms the Thai-Lao border from Chiang Khan in Loei, to Nong Khai, Nakhon Phanom, and Mukdahan provinces before flowing back into Laos at Ubon Ratchathani. The major rivers in the Khorat Basin are the Moon, Chi, Pao, Phong, Prom, Chern, Dome, Young, Lum Plaimart, Phachi, Huai Thabthan, Takhong, Chakkarat, Prasart, Tao, Siaw and Phangchu.

Many of Thailand's important prehistoric sites are found in Isaan and later from the 6th to the 13th century, the area was part of the Khmer empire. Today the region, has some of Thailand's largest cities, but certain important traditions remain.

Isaan Architectural Structures

In the past the area was relatively poor and somewhat isolated from the rest of Thailand. For that reason the area has developed many distinctive beliefs relating to houses and other agricultural structures. Before the mid-twentieth century the area was covered in abundant dry deciduous dipterocarp forests which provided a readily available source of timber. Today, almost one-third of the Thai population lives in Isaan. They belong to diverse ethnic groups, the majority of which are the Tai-Lao speaking groups of the ethnic Thai-Lao, Phu Tai, Saek, Yaw and Yua, who have generally settled in the lowlands. The Mon-Khmer speaking group consists of the Khmer and various ethnic Kha groups such as the Kha Kui (Suay), Kha Lo, Kha Leung, Kha Yer and the Kha Bru.

In the past, members of these two distinct language groups lived quite separately from the others. Thus the Kha Lo and Kha Leung who settled in the forests high on the Phu Pharn Range had little interaction with their neighbours. However, an improved network of roads and communications during the twentieth century has led to an increase in social interaction between different groups which has resulted in mixed settlements, intermarriage, trading and cultural assimilation. Even earlier, however, there were a significant number of Phu Thai groups who preferred to settle on the mountain slopes and in the forest in settlements that were dispersed among the Kha territory. Conversely various Kha ethnic groups moved down from the mountains to join the Thai-Lao lowlanders.

The highland people subsist mainly on hunter-gathering activities and some simple forms of farming. The lowlanders have made their living mainly from agriculture such as in rice and field-crop farming, occasionally supplemented by food gathering in streams, fields, forests and hills. Their settlements have tended to be more clustered and permanent than those of the highlanders. As a result of this lifestyle the Thai-Lao people have developed many unique architectural structures such as the *ruen yai mi khong* (large house with smaller house attached), *ruen yai* (large house), *yao* (temporary house) of various types, *lao khao* (rice granary), *toob tor lao* (a small lean-to attached to the granary), *therb* (a type of hut) and *thieng na* (a rice-field hut). Although less sophisticated than their Central region counterparts, the belief systems associated with Isaan houses and the way in which they reflect the social aspects of Isaan life make them fascinating subjects.

House forms and the Isaan family unit

House types and forms in Isaan are largely determined by the existing family unit, the available building materials and the local technology developed from beliefs and house-building experiences accumulated over time. In the language of Isaan the word *baan* which in the Central region means house, generally refers to the village, while *huen* (the same word as *ruen* in Central Thailand) refers to the individual house.

Previous page: A *ruen yai mi khong* decorated with turned wood at the top of the gable. The stairs are situated on the side. (The Museum of Isaan houses, Maha Sarakham University)

Above: A group of Phu Tai ladies from Kalasin dressed in their best *phasin* and *sabai* to go to the temple.

Above left: Fish traps are woven at home from split bamboo and left out in the many ponds and lakes to be collected in the evening.

Opposite: A so-called *ruen yai* (large house) belonging to Nai Porn Punchit in Nong Chang sub-district, Sam Chai district, Kalasin. In the foreground is a metal ring for calling villagers. The walls of Isaan houses are not prefabricated as in the Central and North, but are simple wooden boards.

Right: A mural from Wat Photaram, Nadoon district, Maha Sarakham province, shows a scene of daily life. In the top right corner, women can be seen spinning silk thread.

Below: This mural painting from the *sim* of Wat Photaram, shows buffaloes ploughing the fields and rice seedlings being transplanted. It should be noted that the main type of rice grown here for domestic consumption is sticky rice.

A *ruen yai* belonging to Nai Chom Punasri in Nong Chang, Kalasin. The gabled roof is tiled, the walls have wooden boards. The underneath of the house can be used for a variety of purposes such as weaving baskets or silk.

House forms reflect the different developmental stages of a family's life cycle, with its oscillations between a stem and a nuclear family. A stem family, consisting of the parents, their children and one son-in-law, reside in a *ruen yai* or *ruen yai mi khong*, a living arrangement that results from the Isaan custom whereby the new son-in-law lives in the house of the wife's parents. After a certain period of time, the married daughter and her husband build their own residence, establishing a separate household and forming a new nuclear family.

Reasons for the split of the stem family could be the desire of the young couple to start their own family, the marriage of another daughter or a conflict between the wife's parents and the son-in-law. Traditionally, only one son-in-law may live in the parents' house, therefore when a new son-in-law came along the old one usually moved out. Before this happened, the couple would normally have had time to accumulate enough materials to build a new house. Then when the time came they would move into the new house, with inherited properties and rice fields from the parents. However, if the couple had to make a sudden move, perhaps following a conflict with the wife's parents, they would normally loose their share in the properties as a punishment for the son-in-law's serious breach of the accepted social norm of unquestionable deference to one's elders.

In the past, the style of house that the couple built after splitting from the stem family would be largely determined by the materials, time and labour they could secure at the time. In the beginning, they might live in a *toob tor lao* (a small lean-to attached to the granary), or one of the various types of *yao*. After a while if all went well the nuclear family would build a more permanent structure such as *ruen yai* or *ruen yai mi khong* in preparation for the expansion into a stem family when a daughter married and brought in a son-in-law, thereby starting another cycle.

This nuclear-to-stem-to-nuclear family cycle relied on the traditional belief in *peung* (the house spirit) as a control mechanism to oversee the son-in-law's conduct. Isaan sons-in-law belong to a different kinship group and, therefore, have a different house spirit. They were accepted into the wife's family because of the labour they contributed to such agricultural activities as rice and field-crop farming and *sao na* (the clearing of forest land for additional rice fields). The ritual of raising a house-spirit shelf (*hing peung*) at the back wall of the new house after splitting from the parents symbolized the family's independence as an economic and social unit. It announced the beginning of a new family, which would develop into a stem family with a permanent house of their own in the near future.

In the old days, the newly-split nuclear family would begin to accumulate timber and other materials for the building of a more permanent *ruen yai* or *ruen yai mi khong*, a task usually accomplished well before the eldest daughter reached a marrying age. Attitudes

A *ruen yai* within the village of Panna Nikhom, Sakon Nakhon. In the background may be seen a granary with no wall panels.

Families who weave silk often keep silkworms in *kradong* on shelves inside the house. The silkworms, which are provided with mosquito nets, live on mulberry leaves, before spinning their cocoons. Na Kao, Vapee-pathum district, Maha Sarakham province.

Above: A young girl is weaving a *prae wa* cloth used as a kind of shoulder scarf.

Right: This lady is preparing cotton underneath her house in Chiang Khan, Loei.

reflecting the practice of matrilocal residence after marriage can be summed up in the saying:

Bringing in a son-in-law to look after the parents is like filling a granary with rice;

Bringing in a daughter-in-law to look after the family elders is like filling the house with sinister spirits.

This clearly reflects the importance attached to the son-in-law's labour in the fields. Daughters-in-law were prohibited from living with the husband's family for fear of the conflicts which might arise between mother and daughter-in-law. Traditionally, daughters should stay with their own mothers so they could be properly trained and supervised in their housewifely duties. In a matrilocal living arrangement, the sons-in-law tended to have fewer problems with their in-laws as they normally spent most of the day working in the fields, away from the house, and were not constantly in contact with other members of the household.

Agricultural activities are not confined to men however. During the rice planting and harvesting season, women also take part. At other times, most Isaan women are involved in weaving or basket making underneath the house. Cotton trees are often grown in the compound or village, while silkworms are raised and fed on mulberry leaves. When the cocoons are ready the silk is spun into thread before being woven into cloths for men (*pakama*) or lengths for women to make into skirts. Dies can come from a variety of natural materials such as bark, indigo, fruits and beetles.

An old Isaan lady is spinning thread before beginning weaving in Na Kao village, Vapeepathum district, Maha Sarakham.

Ruen yai mi khong (large house with small house)

This is a large three-room house built entirely of hardwood with balk posts. It represents the ideal Isaan house form. The *khong* or *ruen noi* (small house) built parallel with the length of the main house, is similar to the twin house of the Central region. The difference between the *ruen yai* and *ruen noi* is, as their name makes clear, their relative size; the latter is always smaller or lower than the large house. Depending on the availability of materials and its intended usage, the *ruen noi* may be built to the same design as the *ruen yai*, including the wall panels and surrounding balustrades.

A corridor connects the *ruen yai* and *ruen noi* which are built as two separate structures. Sometimes the two houses and the connecting corridor are built on a single level; at other times the corridor is on the same level as the *ruen yai* but higher than the *ruen noi*; and sometimes it is on the same level as the *ruen noi*, but lower than the *ruen yai*. A *harng rin* (gutter) runs along the two adjacent eaves to prevent rainwater from ruining the corridor.

The interior of the *ruen yai* is generally partitioned into three rooms. The partitions may run from post to post, to midway between the posts, or to a third post set up to support partition panels extending out from the two original posts. At later periods, it was popular to leave the northern or eastern room with no partition panels at all.

All three rooms in the *ruen yai* have specific functions. The northern or eastern room is usually designated as the *hong peung* (room for the house spirit). In the old days, this room was known as *hua ruen* (head of the house) because the shelf for the house spirit, a symbol of authority and house ownership, was set up on its back wall or corner post. It is sometimes used as a bedroom for the male family members and was off-limits to the sons-in-law. The room on the western or the southern side of the house is called the *hong suam* or *thaii ruen* (the end of the house). This is the daughters' bedroom which a married daughter shares with her husband and, thus, is also known as the *bawn nawn phii aai* (the elder brother-in-law's bedroom). When a brother-in-law joins the household the younger sisters have to sleep in the *hong klang* (the central room), formerly the parents' bedroom, who either move out to sleep on a verandah in front of the *hong klang*, to the *hong peung* or sometimes to the more spacious *ruen noi* instead.

Apart from being used as sleeping quarters for the parents, the *ruen noi* is used as a guest bedroom or a multi-purpose room for guests, working or storage. If necessary, it can be partitioned off into a bedroom or a kitchen. One end of the connecting corridor between the two houses is generally extended, at a lower level, as an open deck or as a stairway platform. The deck is sometimes extended into a verandah running the whole width of the house.

Above left: A *ruen yai mi khong* in hardwood throughout. Here the smaller size of the *khong* is clearly visible.

Above middle: A shelf for the Buddha image is frequently placed against a corner post, which is usually the northern or eastern corner.

Above right: The roof structure of a *ruen yai mi khong*. A small ventilation panel is visible near the top of the gable end.

The verandah of a *ruen yai mi khong* is used for all kinds of purposes. The gables are in the ubiquitous sunburst pattern. (The Museum of Isaan Houses, Maha Sarakham University)

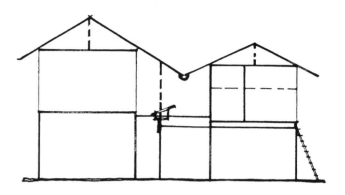

Ruen yai (a large house)

A *ruen yai* is built entirely of hardwood with balk posts. Similar to the *ruen yai mi khong*, it is a three-room house with high-pitched roof and gable ends. Its interior is similarly partitioned into the *hong peung*, the parents' room and the married daughter and son-in-law's bedroom. The only difference between the two types is the presence or absence of the *khong* or *ruen noi*. With the *ruen yai*, the *ruen noi* is replaced by an extended verandah at a lower elevation, whose floor joists are attached to the notches on the existing house posts or to extra posts next to the old ones. Sometimes more posts are raised at the outer edges to support a *koey* (a lean-to roof projecting from under the house eaves) covering the extended verandah. The outer edge of the verandah is normally fitted with horizontal railings or full panels, but it may also be left uncovered. The stairway is placed midway along this verandah.

In the past the pitched roof and *koey* were usually covered by thatched grass. However, houses built near forests and mountains had roofs covered with hardwood shingles. Although more difficult to make, these were more durable than grass.

At later periods, another section of verandah might be added to the front of the *ruen yai* supported by joists attached to the existing verandah posts. Sometimes separate posts of 1.00-1.50 metres were added and horizontal railings were fitted to these posts for hanging

Right: Basket weaving is frequently done by older members of the household. Here, in the house of Porn Punchit, the old man is weaving a basket to hold sticky rice.

Far right: The bed in an Isaan house is often a multi-purpose piece of furniture which is turned into a bed in the evening, the bedclothes being stored in the bed/chest during the day. (Chom Punasri house, Nong Chang sub-district, Kalasin)

clothes. A *harng ang nam*, a shelf at the same level as the railings, was sometimes constructed to house the earthenware drinking water jars. Other large jars of water for household use were placed in a row along the verandah edge. A section of this verandah was also set aside for a kitchen. The cooking platform, *mae ding fai*, was an earth-filled square timber frame with three *kon sao* (a lump of clay or rock) forming the bases for cooking pots.

The space beneath the house was used for a number of purposes – keeping animals, spinning and weaving, or simply relaxing and entertaining guests.

Traditionally, a *ruen yai* was the ideal for a stem family and a symbol of that family's success. The goal of Isaan people to own a *ruen yai* is seen in the saying:

"To be happy is to always have rice for consumption, a piece of land to live on, a good spouse to share one's bed, a purse full of gold, a ruen yai with wooden shingles, and a lot of caring offspring".

Above: An elderly lady is making her meal in a typical Isaan-style kitchen, with split bamboo walls to provide good ventilation.

Left: An Isaan meal usually comprises vegetables, fish and sticky rice. Small bananas, tamarind pods and herbs are also arranged on the tray.

Left: In the foreground a tall rice granary with split bamboo walls and in the backround two *yao,* one with leaf thatch and the other with grass.

Below: A *ruen yai* in which the front verandah extends beyond the eaves. The steps leaning against the verandah are typical of the Isaan style.

Opposite: This *ruen yai* has the kitchen on the left-hand side. The latter has louvred windows and split bamboo walls. The underneath of the house is being used to house livestock.

Right: A man in Kalasin is making a roof out of *Imperator* grass.

Far right: Woven mats are used for wall panels and floors.

Below: A *toob yao* is used for a single family or as a temporary dwelling. It is roofed with grass and has woven bamboo walls. (The Museum of Isaan Houses, Maha Sarakham University)

Yao (various temporary structures)

Nowadays the word *yao* is seldom used as it has almost become synonymous with the word *ruen* as used in the phrase *yao ruen*. However, in Isaan 'yao' is still used to refer to specific architectural structures, whose forms vary with family size, duration of habitation, social status and physical environment.

Yao refers to various types of one-story structure built mainly of wood and raised on posts in a similar style to the *ruen yai* and *ruen yai mi khong*, although the posts are not necessarily balk posts. The *yao* differs, however, in having only two rooms and an extended lower level verandah at the front. Its pitched roof with gable ends extends either to cover both the house and the verandah or only the house, while a lean-to roof or *keoy* is added to cover the verandah. Not nearly as refined as the *ruen yai*, the *yao* is built with rough and more perishable components. The largest type is called a *dunk tang khan*. Most *yao* have the *sao ek* in the middle supporting the ridge beam. The outer walls are either planks or split woven bamboo panels. The interior is partitioned to provide one bedroom. The other room, at the head of the stairway, is left open or sometimes temporarily partitioned with a door, and is used as storage or as the children's sleeping quarters. A house-spirit shelf is sometimes raised in a ceremony to mark the ownership of the *yao*.

The covered verandah is used for resting, dining or entertaining guests. It may be extended on the opposite

edge to the stairway to set up a cooking area. Often, however, the cooking is often done on the ground in front of, or next to, the steps.

Generally, a *yao* is the residence of a nuclear family who have moved out of a *ruen yai* or *ruen yai mi khong* of the wife's family. It is a temporary dwelling usually built on the wife's inherited piece of land. The new family may still be connected socially to the stem family but the move symbolises economic and ritual independence epitomised in the raising of a separate house-spirit shelf. Eventually it may evolve into a three-room *ruen yai* or *ruen yai mi khong*.

Toob yao or dunk tor din style of yao
This is a two-room temporary hut for a nuclear family similar to the *dunk tang khan* style of *yao*, but smaller and lower, sitting on 0.80-1.20 metre-high wooden posts. The rest of the structural framework is also wooden, partly tied together by twine or vines. Grass thatch is used for the roof covering and woven-leaf or bamboo mats for the walls. The floor is made of flattened bamboo stems. The interior is partitioned into a bedroom and storage area, with a small opening against which a three-step ladder is rested.

The overall structure is not very strong and, therefore, a central pole is sunk into the ground to support the ridge beam bracing the roof beams which support the weight of the rafters or ridge boards. This is called the *dunk*, hence the name *dunk tor din*.

When a nuclear family splits from the stem family it may build a *dunk tang khan yao* right away. But if the spilt is quite sudden due to an unforeseen event such as an unscheduled marriage of the wife's sister or a quarrel between the parents and son-in-law, the nuclear family may have to settle for a temporary hut in the *toob yao* or *dunk tor din* style. Real wood flooring, when available, can be used in place of *fark* (split bamboo), but in this case more care is necessary in the construction as the *yao* has to be strong enough to support the extra weight.

In the old days such a *yao* could be completed in a single day with the help of only two to three people. The owner might ask other men to cut down trees in the forest and rice-fields, or he could use tree trunks already felled while clearing the fields for rice-growing. Then the family could take another one to three years to accumulate enough material to build a *dunk tang khan yao* or a *ruen yai*.

A roof extension is usually added to the front of the *toob yao* with an incline down to 1.50-2.00 metres, sometimes to cover a raised platform. The area is generally used for storing tools and kitchen utensils. Because a *toob yao* is a small temporary shelter with a low floor, a hearth is usually set up for cooking under the outer edge of the roof.

Above left: A *toob yao* with woven bamboo walls and a thatch and corrugated-iron roof.

Above: A *toob yao* in Kuchinarai, Kalasin province. The roof is grass mixed with a few wooden planks, while the walls are woven bamboo.

Opposite: A wooden granary with a corrugated iron roof in the compound of Home Tingkodorn, Na Kao sub-district, Vapeepathum district.

Right and far right: Two *toob tor lao* which show how the adjoining platform can either be almost the same height or significantly lower.

The lao khao (rice granary)

Lao khao refers to a rice granary, a building central to the Isaan livelihood where rice-growing activities are closely related to kinship and communal relationships. It is also intertwined with such ceremonies as *sukhwan lao* (a ceremony to console the spiritual essence of the rice granary), and its construction clearly reflects many ancient beliefs.

An Isaan granary consists of two-three small rooms of 1.20 x 2.00 metres. All the posts and structural components of the granary are hardwood while the walls are made of reeds (found in abundance near local ponds) woven into mats, or sometimes woven bamboo panels. The panels are coated with mud mixed with cow or buffalo dung to prevent rice grains from lodging in grooves or falling through any holes. Latterly more durable wooden panels have replaced these types.

The granary roof is pitched with gable ends about one metre high. The pitch prevents rainwater from trickling through a thatched roof. The floor is made of hardwood planks laid tightly together and the gaps sealed with small strips of wood to prevent grain leak. The floor slopes, with the back being about 10-15 cm higher than the front section to compensate for any extra weight, since the granary is always filled from back to front and thus has to bear additional weight. The sloping floor also facilitates the unloading of the rice as the slope pushes the remaining rice towards the front opening.

In the past the granary door was made of horizontal planks placed into grooved frames on both sides, the number of planks needed depending on the amount of rice in store. Gaps between the planks were covered with mats to prevent spillage. The *charn lao*, an extended wooden platform protruding 50-80 cm, was built in front of the door as a ledge for rice containers. The granary steps are a ladder (*kern*) made of bamboo sections or tree boughs with branches for rungs. The number of rice granaries in a house compound reflects the family's wealth and social standing within the community. It may also be used as an indicator of the amount of rice fields, cows and buffaloes owned by a particular family, as well as of the hard-working nature of family members.

There are a large number of traditional religious beliefs and rituals associated with the granary. For example, there is a ritual in which certain leaves and flowers are offered to the granary to *kham khoon*, to ensure sufficient yields for consumption and trade. The offerings are tucked into the outer walls. Another belief involves a restriction against taking the rice out of the granary, once it is harvested and stored, between the first and second lunar month. It can be removed only after the *sukhwan lao* ceremony has been performed on the third day of the new moon of the third lunar month. During this ceremony offerings of food and sweets are placed on the top of the rice pile in the granary. Other traditions involve the interpretation

Once the rice has been harvested but before the unhusked rice is stored there will a ceremony for the spirit of the granary. The leaves of the *khoon, yor and kled lin* are inserted into spaces around the granary posts.

Above: Children playing in front of their *lao khao* in Khon Kaen province.

Below: Villagers are filling up the granary with unhusked rice.

of thunder, known as *fah khai pratoo nam* (the sky opening a water gate), as an omen for next year's rainfall; a *sukhwan* ceremony to console the working animals; and *sukhwan* rite for the community elders.

Toob tor lao (a lean-to extension of the granary)

This aesthetically somewhat unremarkable lateral extension of the granary is nevertheless highly significant in understanding Isaan family life.

A *toob tor lao* is a temporary raised and covered platform built at the side of the granary. It is supported by the existing granary posts on one side and by three to four new wooden posts, depending on the size of the granary, on the other. In the past the landing was covered with thatched grass or wood shingles,

which today have been replaced by corrugated iron or asbestos corrugated tiles. The *toob tor lao* is quite low and can be reached by a three-rung ladder. This type of hut is a temporary residence for a nuclear family; the cooking area is simply placed on the ground in the front. When a similar hut is built on the ground next to the granary without a raised platform as a storage area to keep tools and implements, it is called a *therb*. This is an important distinction and the designation *toob tor lao* is used only when a raised platform structure is built as a family dwelling.

In the past this relatively modest structure did not necessarily signify family poverty because the existence of a granary was already an indicator of wealth, as only ownership of a certain amount of land and a number of animals would justify its construction. A *toob tor lao* was usually built following some unexpected event, usually the sudden marriage of a younger daughter, which entailed an immediate split of the stem family. It was only a temporary residence before the married daughter and her husband could acquire enough wood to build a more permanent *dunk tang khan yao* or *ruen yai*. In other cases a *toob tor lao* served as an interim dwelling while the nuclear family who had moved out and lived in a *toob yao* for some time had dismantled it and were building a *ruen yai*. If the hut had enough space the children might also live there, but they usually stayed with the grandparents until the new house was finished.

Thieng na (rice-field huts)

This is another type of temporary hut similar in appearance to a *toob yao* built on a *don hua na* (a mound in the rice-fields). Such mounds were believed to be where the field spirits reside. When forest was cleared for the rice-fields the spirits could be angry and a tradition evolved of engaging in mock verbal abuse before putting up a *thieng na* in order to drive any spirits away. The name *thieng na* was derived from the verbal fight or *thieng* performed at the site.

Generally, the whole family will live in a *thieng na* during the rice-growing season, which usually lasts four to six months a year, from ploughing through to the seedling transplanting. After planting, the family will move back to the village and visit the *thieng na* from time to time. They will move to the *thieng na* again during harvest and threshing, returning to the village once the rice has been stored in the granary around the first or second lunar month.

People with rice-fields located far from the village face a long trek to their fields. They have to spend a long period each year in the *thieng na*. Many make some improvements to their shacks to render them more secure and comfortable, to such an extent that they often become more like an ordinary *toob yao* than a field hut. When a group of neighbouring farmers establish more and more 'improved' *thieng na*, the area becomes transformed into a new community and their shelters will then be known as *thieng yao*.

Top left and right: Typical *thieng na* stand in the middle of the rice fields.

Above: An aerial view of rice fields. Trees are left to provide shade and wood once they attain a certain size.

Traditional Beliefs

The more traditional Isaan structures such as the *ruen yai mi khong*, *ruen yai*, *yao*, *lao khao* and *thieng na* are richly endowed with elaborate beliefs and superstitions. There are beliefs about the selection of building materials, the auspicious times for house building, the appropriate direction and location of the house, the correct stages for house building as well as the appropriate manner for carrying out house improvements and dismantling procedures. In addition, there are a large variety of prescriptions and taboos to be observed concerning these matters.

The *ruen yai* and *ruen yai mi khong* were the ideal houses for an Isaan family in the old days, when a stem family lived together permanently. Isaan houses are built by their male inhabitants. In the past the labour was usually provided by relatives and neighbours. Other jobs were also clearly segregated along gender lines. Tilling the fields, tending the fruit trees and looking after animals was the task of men, while women helped in certain areas such as transplanting rice seedlings and harvesting. Men needed to know how to build houses, weave baskets and certain household goods, hammer out knives and scythes, while women spun thread and wove textiles, carried water and pounded rice.

The building of a *ruen yai* was an important affair and good preparation was necessary. For example, tree trunks of 'good character' were acquired to ensure good fortune for the family. These were straight tree

Right: Chiang Khan villagers give food to the monks during their early morning alms round.

Far right: Two elderly Kalasin ladies dressed in their best *phasin* and *sabai* to go to the temple.

Opposite above: The east wall within the bedroom. The wall at the head of the bed usually has a shelf for the Buddha image and other sacred items. Here there is a statue of His Majesty the King and the ashes of the family ancestors. (Porn Punchit's house, Nong Chang sub-district, Kalasin)

Opposite left: The shelf in the *hua ruen* with a small Buddha image in Isaan style. Cotton and an hibiscus flower have been placed as offerings.

trunks of the appropriate size with few dead knots. Sometimes one chose a perfect tree in the forest by listening to the rustling of the leaves of each tree in the middle of the night to decide whether the sounds were commendable. If so, they would mark the trees and return to fell them afterwards with help from family and neighbours. One also had to ask for permission from the spirit of the tree. Various trees are unsuitable for house posts, for example, those with entwined vines, trees with a hollow trunk, or trees which had been struck by lightening.

Once the trees suitable for the house posts had been obtained, they would be trimmed into balk posts. An old Isaan saying concerning this practice states that: "*hark sao bor pen liam khao saen si kliang kor bor ngarm*", meaning that a post not trimmed into a balk post is considered unattractive, no matter how smooth it is. Other undesirable posts are those of inappropriate length, posts with a knot right below where a beam will rest, and posts with a knot at the same height as a domesticated pig. These posts were believed to bring bad luck.

The timing for cutting the trees was also important and it was believed that wood should only be felled in the first four months of the year. After this time the wood is in a spiritual state and should not be cut.

Because the posts were hewn by several different hands they might not all be of the same dimensions. Accordingly the look and size of the posts were also used as omens: those posts which had the same thickness along the entire length were very good, while those where the base of post was thick and the top thinner were simply good.

The site for the house should be open and flat, with no holes in the ground, small ponds or termite mounds. Once a suitable plot has been found the *kum khun* of the ground is also assessed. In the past three banana leaf bowls [*kratong*] of white, black and brown sticky rice were left in the centre of the plot for the crows to peck. If the crows chose the black sticky rice, the site was unsuitable, if they chose the red it was extremely inauspicious, while the choice of the white sticky rice meant that the occupants would enjoy a long and happy life in a house on that spot.

As in all the different regions of Thailand, certain times are favourable and others unfavourable for house construction. The fourth month will ensure a happy household, building in the sixth month will bring riches and many friends, while building in the ninth month will ensure an ever-full rice granary.

Building on a Monday will bring textiles two months later and riches. Building on a Wednesday will bring consumable goods and textiles. Building on a Thursday will bring happiness and after five months much good fortune.

In the past it was believed that if the house was erected in the first three months the *sao hek* should be raised to the northeast to ensure a prosperous life for

Above left: The *sao hek* is decorated with cotton during construction. Here the main structural frame of the house is almost completed.

Above right: A set of steps at a house in Maha Sarakham. There must be an uneven number of steps which are round and inserted into holes in the stringers before being secured with nails.

the owner. In the fourth to sixth months the post should be raised towards the southeast. In the seventh to ninth months, the auspicious direction moved to the southwest, while in the 10th-12th months the post should be raised towards the northwest.

Holes for the house posts are dug prior to their being placed nearby in readiness for the ceremony to erect the *sao hek* and *sao khwan* (equivalent to the *sao ek* and *sao tho* of the Central region), which had to be performed at an auspicious time. On the day of the ceremony the owner of the house must wake in the early hours of the morning to carry the *nam kon ka* (water obtained before the crow) to water the bottom of the pits for the two main posts. At an auspicious time the neighbours helped to lower the posts into the postholes. Each post would be given names believed to bring good luck to the house. For example, a post may be named *kham* (gold), *khoon* (prosperity), *mi* (wealthy), or *man* (firm or permanent).

The steps of the house are second in importance only to the house posts. Again the hardwood chosen must not have any knots and must be able to withstand the sun and rain. The stairs must include the following components: the father stringer, the mother stringer, and the child steps. The father stringer is to the right of the stairway and must be longer than the mother one. The steps have to have an odd number of treads as an even number is associated with the dead.

The planks used for the floor of the house are hardwoods such as *mai daeng*, *mai teng* or *pradu* (*Pterocarpus macrocarpus*). The length of the planks should be the same as the width of the room.

Apart from the long list of things that needed to be done before and during house building, there are also many prohibitions regarding house construction: Houses must not be built on the site of disused ponds. No pond must be filled in order to build a house and houses should not be built in marshy areas. Houses must not be built over a large tree stump, nor over a termite mound.

Two separate houses must not be joined into one as this will bring bad luck. A house must not be reduced in size down to a shack. A house must not be dismantled and reassembled in the same day. A house must not have an extension coming out from the centre of the long wall as this is most inauspicious.

There are also prohibitions regarding the directional siting of a house. The gable of the house should face towards the east or the west (*long tawan*). If the gable faces north or south (*kwang tawan*) it is believed that great misfortune will ensue.

When the house was finished a housewarming ceremony was organized before the owners would take up residency. The ceremony was a combination of Brahministic and Buddhist ritual presided over by a *moh tham* and by Buddhist monks, respectively.

The three auspicious days for taking up residence in a new house are: Wednesday, Thursday and Friday.

Before the ceremonies start the owner of the house must prepare the following items: *kub koeng* (a broad-brimmed hat from palm leaves; a cotton bag with tools, a lump of silver, gold and copper; a net with gold and silver fishes and a smaller net to spoon up fish; a sword; nails or chisel or a plane; spirits; bedclothes and clothes; household utensils; an offering tray made from a banana leaf; a sharpening stone; a bowl of flowers with candles and joss-sticks; a water jar; a rice storage jar; leaves of the *khoon* and *yor* trees.

On the day of the ceremony the people are divided into two groups. The 'owner group' of two or three people cut a fresh banana leaf to put at the bottom of the steps held in place with the sharpening stone. They then stand at the top of the stairs on the house. The other group, including village elders, young men and women and children, carry the aforementioned objects to the house in a procession. The leader, wearing a hat or holding an umbrella, also has the cotton bag containing the various items over his shoulder. The procession circles the house three times in a clockwise direction, singing, dancing and playing musical instruments, before finishing up at the foot of the steps. The leader then ascends to the house where the 'owners' greet them, holding the offerings and candles, joss-sticks and flowers. The leader lights the candles and putting his hands together in prayer he sits down on a stone to pray to the gods of direction and ask that the owners will have a happy life in the house.

The hosts then invite the guests into the house to participate in the wall-knocking ritual where each person knocks once on the wall while uttering a propitious phrase. Each person leaves a bag containing such things as money, flowers, and candles which will bring good luck to the occupants. A ritual of mock sleeping-in follows with an elderly couple pretending to sleep on the prepared mat and bedding to be awakened by the roosters at dawn. The couple then relate the good dreams they have had during their sleep. After the ceremonies a feast is given both in the house and underneath.

Above: Monks having their lunch of sticky rice in a forest clearing.

Below: Monks having their lunch at a villager's house during the Songkran festival, which takes place during April. As well as being the traditional Thai New Year, this festival is believed to bring on the rains and is held at the end of the dry season.

Above right: An Isaan-style spirit house with a sunburst gable.

Above: People pouring water on the Buddha images in the compound of a temple during the Songkran festival. Villagers will take them out only for this occasion to mark the new year. The Songkran festival is celebrated throughout Thailand but especially in the Northeast.

The room on the eastern or northern side of the house (depending in which direction it faces), or *hong peung* is designated as the *hua ruen* (head of the house). It is also the *hong phi* (the spirit room) into which sons-in-law may not enter. This taboo is also extended to the cases where the daughters-in-law have moved in with their husband's family. The daughters-in-law are also forbidden to pass the room while simply wearing a sarong and must not scold or hit the children in that spot. These taboos are sanctioned by the whole community. Their violation has to be rectified by a *somma* ritual in which the violator asks for forgiveness from the ancestor spirits in front of the parents, relatives and neighbours. Failing to perform this ritual will mean that the violators cannot remain in the same house as the parents.

Ruen yai and *ruen yai mi khong* are the permanent home of a stem family and when the whole family may have to leave the house for an extended period to tend the faraway fields or to clear new plots of land, the house is considered deserted. It is believed that once the occupants desert the house, ghosts and spirits will take over. However, such an undesirable situation can be prevented by a simple ceremony of informing the house spirits of the temporary vacancy; a mortar and pestle are left in the house to fool any bad spirits into thinking that the house is occupied at all times.

An old *ruen yai* that has stood for decades may degenerate and be downgraded to a *yao* or temporary

house. If a new *ruen yai* is to be built the old one must be taken down first. Parts of the old house can be re-used and go through a new house raising ceremony. Apart from taboos regarding construction, there are also strict beliefs regarding repairs. If a section of roof needs repair, the whole house has to be dismantled, as it is believed that repairing the roof while the house is standing will bring bad fortune. Such a house is known as a *ruen hua kard* (a house without a head). In contrast, if only the floor or the walls need repairs, they can be carried out in situ. Nevertheless, the floors and walls cannot be planed without first taking the planks apart, as this results in a botched job. Houses repaired in such a fashion are called *ruen lork klarb* (a peeling house).

There are fewer restrictions and taboos concerning the *yao*, *lao khao* and *thieng na* because of their temporary nature. A spirit shelf raising ceremony in a *yao* is a simple affair compared to a similar ceremony in a *ruen yai*.

Although various ceremonies are carried out in connection with the rice and the granary, its construction is relatively simple and strictures were confined to choosing a suitable location in relation to the *ruen yai* and the wind direction, so that rice dust would not blow to the main house. In addition, during the period when the harvested rice was being loaded into the granary the women of the house had to bring rice from the granary to pound in the rice pounder everyday.

Large trees are often associated with sprits and sometimes spirit houses are built near them as the spirit house for the whole community.

Above: Isaan temples, such as Wat Phochai in Kalasin, are relatively simple when compared with their Central region or Northern counterparts.

Right: This small *sim* in Wat Sri Than has a corrugated iron three-tiered roof.

Far right: This *kantoey* shows the earth goddess, Toranee, squeezing her hair to provide water.

Chapter 4
The South

All the four regions of Thailand have their particular character, but the South may be one of the most distinctive. Part of the reason is undoubtedly due to the fact that the region is a peninsular rather than a land mass. With sea on both sides, over the centuries the South became an important juncture between the two great influences on Southeast Asia – India and China. Important trading entrepots grew up and during the 7th century Srivijaya was a significant city state, as archaeological finds attest. Many wrecks in the Gulf of Thailand have been found to contain large shipments of Chinese porcelain.

Linked with trade, was the introduction of new religions, first Buddhism and later Islam. Today both religions coexist peacefully and find material expression in the art and architecture of the South. While the ten provinces of Chumphon, Ranong, Surat Thani, Phang Nga, Nakhon Si Thammarat, Phuket, Krabi, Trang, Patthalung and Songkhla are predominantly Buddhist and have an architecture, both religious and secular, closely allied with Central Thailand, the four southernmost provinces of Yala, Satun, Narathiwat and Pattani are 70% Muslim and, as such, have developed a distinctive culture and architecture of their own. Although similarities with other Thai traditional houses may be discerned, the importance of the influence of Malaysian, or even Indonesian, architecture cannot be overlooked. In addition, the requirements of Muslim families to pray five times a day and to have family members close by has resulted in house plans which differ from those elsewhere.

Maritime Influences

The southern region of Thailand is endowed with rich natural resources and magnificent scenery from the spectacular cliffs of its innumerable continuous mountain ranges to the panoramic seascapes along its eastern coast on the Gulf of Thailand and the western coast on the Andaman Sea. Its year-round, lush greenery is a result of the hot and humid tropical climate with a high level of rainfall that makes southern Thailand very suitable for rubber and fruit plantations.

Social and cultural characteristics

The population of the South comprises peoples of diverse ethnicity, culture, and religious beliefs with a long history of harmonious co-existence. Buddhism and Islam are the two major religions in the region. The Chinese, who have been settled in the South since the Ayutthaya period, brought with them vibrant cultural elements which have since been incorporated into the local culture, generating a characteristically Southern way of life. Another well-known ethnic group is the *Chao Lay*, or the sea gypsies, and the Sakai indigenous people who live in small groups preserving their traditional way of life and certain aspects of their cultural heritage. Apart from the local inhabitants, the region has seen a constant influx of traders and seafarers. It is this diverse mix of peoples who have created a unique southern vernacular architectural tradition manifested in their houses, Buddhist temples, Islamic mosques, palaces and public buildings.

Above: Muslim women at an early morning market typical of those found in the south.

Left: A communal well within the compound of a Muslim house. In the background sheets of rubber are drying in the sun.

Previous page: The Thai style house in the grounds of Patthalung palace.

Left: Part of Songkhla lake viewed from Koh Yor in Songkhla. Local villagers build their houses on stilts over the water and raise sea bass in the fish cages.

Below: Two Sakai women from Tarn Toh district, Yala province.

Middle: The Sakai are a small group of indigenous people inhabiting Southern Thailand. They hunt using long blow pipes and mainly live in Tarn Toh district, Yala province.

Bottom: A Muslim school is situated in the grounds of Wadi Al-Hussein mosque in Bajoh, Narathiwat.

Samui in Surat Thani is a large island with hills rising to over 600 metres. Being near the equator it has a tropical climate with abundant rainfall throughout the year and rich vegetation.

Geographical features

Geographically, the southern peninsular is located between the South China Sea (in the Pacific Ocean) on the east and the Andaman Sea (in the Indian Ocean) on the west. The peninsular, which in places is extremely narrow, is formed by three mountain ranges: to the north is the lower end of the Tanao Sri Range or the Phuket Range; in the middle is the Khao Luang or Nakhon Si Thammarat Range; and to the south is the San Kalakhiri Range. The limestone has eroded over millennia to form steep cliffs and dramatic landscapes both on land and in the form of islands off the coast. A large lake with access to the sea has formed at Songkhla and is home to numerous birds.

The south has a hot tropical climate with high humidity and precipitation from both the western and eastern monsoons, with the north-east monsoon blowing from September to November and the south-west monsoon from May to October; storms and high winds are common all year round. There are only two seasons, the hot and rainy seasons. The climate is suitable for agriculture with the region's major crops being rubber and tropical fruits such as durian and mangosteen. Large coconut groves now ring the shoreline which in earlier times would have been fringed with mangrove and nipa palms.

The influence of these geographical and climatic features on the vernacular architectural style of the South will be discussed in later sections.

Left: Wat Phra Barommathat, Chaiya, Surat Thani. Some historians believe that Chaiya was the centre of the Srivijayan kingdom.

Below: A bronze Avalokitesvara originally with four arms, from Chaiya district, Surat Thani. It dates to the 9th century AD and shows Indian Pala influence. (National Museum, Bangkok)

Below right: Such images of Buddha sheltered by *naga* are relatively rare in Srivijayan art. (National Museum, Bangkok)

Historical background

To fully understand the nature and origin of the region's vernacular architecture, it is essential that we consider southern local history.

The areas around the Bay of Phang Nga have some of the oldest settlements in Thailand. Archaeological evidence of flake and polished stone tools and charred remains discovered in the area attest to the presence of prehistoric human settlements dating back to over 27,000 years ago.

During the 1st and 2nd centuries AD and the 7th century AD, various entrepots grew up on the Southern peninsular to serve the maritime trade routes. It was through their trade partners, who came mainly from India and China, that Buddhism and Hinduism, the two major religious systems underlying the distinct cultural elements and art forms of the South, were introduced to the region.

During the 6th and 7th centuries AD, Srivijaya, an entrepot on the Chinese trade route, gained in prosperity and political significance as a powerful coastal state. However by the 13th century, Srivijaya was in decline following a change in policy in which China broke the trade monopoly previously enjoyed by the state. Then the 14th century rise of Ayutthaya in the Central region saw all the outlying parts of Thailand losing their importance as trading centres.

However, for at least a millennium the Southern region's history reflected a continuous flow of foreign

Right: The building housing the National Museum in Songkhla was formerly the palace of the governor. It was built by Phraya Suntranurak (Netra na Songkhla) in 1878. It combines Chinese influence in the roofs and western stylistic features such as the curving central staircase.

Below: The underside of the verandah roof has wooden beams in Chinese-style.

Vernacular Southern Architecture

As with traditional houses in other regions of Thailand, certain key characteristics are shared, while the details are different. Thus, houses in the South are mostly wooden and are raised on posts to a height just above an adult's head, enabling the area beneath the house to be used for resting, storage, animal shelter and occupational-related activities such as making bird cages or weaving grass (*krajood*) mats. As with the Central region, various elements of the house are prefabricated and assembled on the site. Panels of wood, bamboo matting or corrugated iron are used for the walls, and local materials such as grass and palm thatch are used for the roof coverings. As we have also seen elsewhere, the houses can be divided into two basic types: the *ruen krueng sab* (houses built mainly of wood) and *ruen krueng pook* (houses tied together with rope or twine).

The architectural features commonly found in Southern houses are as follows:

1. High-pitched roofs which allow the abundant rainfall to run of quickly. Such roofs can be classified into three main styles: gabled, hipped and the so-called Manila style of hipped roof. A further feature, also reflecting the heavy driving rain, is the deep overhanging eaves which extend to cover the stairways.

2. Instead of being buried in the ground, house posts customarily rest on hardwood footings, or in recent years on concrete pillars. This is because the ground is always damp and wooden posts would rot.

3. Each component of the house is prefabricated on site before being assembled in order to facilitate possible relocation of the house in the future.

4. Fruit trees, such as coconut, mango, jackfruit or banana are planted in lieu of a fence to provide shade and mark the house boundary.

5. The house is oriented towards the road or waterway to catch the sea breeze. This practice results in the uniquely southern tradition of pointing one's head towards the south while sleeping.

In the past, vernacular architecture was not designed with such specific purposes in mind as is common today. The occupants usually built their own houses with the help of their neighbours and local carpenters, or sometimes with carpenters or labourers hired from nearby villages. House forms were determined by the occupants' needs, coupled with the customs, beliefs, building traditions and materials of each locality. They reflect the owner's cultural background, attitudes and taste, as well as his or her social and economic standing within the community. It is the synthesis of different aspects of local culture that makes such architecture most attractive.

The traditional architecture of the South can be classified by function into four categories: religious, commercial (shops below with living space above), residential and public structures such as city pillars, *chedis*, reliquary monuments, schools, pavilions, shadow puppet theatre halls, etc.

Above: A group of houses with gable ends in the form of a sunburst stand in the grounds of the Southern Educational Institute, Songkhla province.

Above middle: The interior of the roof space of the Wadi Al-Hussein mosque shows a *dunk* carved with *nom maew* flowers.

Above left: A typical *teen sao*, or post base, in this case of concrete. Such posts can withstand the damp conditions and attacks by termites.

Right: A Muslim house with a *panya*-style roof. Note the columns of coconuts piled up against the side of the house.

Below right: A Southern house in Barahao sub-district with a large twin-gabled roof and a smaller one over the projecting porch.

Top left: A twin-gabled Muslim house in Yaring district. The wood panelled walls facing onto the canal show some Central Thai influence.

Top right: One of these twin houses in Satun province has woven mat walls while the other uses horizontal wooden boards.

Above left: This simple, single-gabled house in Satun uses woven mats for the gable as well as the wall panels.

Above right: A twin-gabled Muslim house with sunburst gable panels. Note the ventilation panels at the top of the walls and above the windows.

Above: Two locals ride a tricyle past a typical shophouse in Pattani in the early morning. Note the stucco detailing on the side of the projecting roof.

Left: The Wadi Al-Hussein mosque in Pattani province is the oldest such structure in Thailand. It was built in 1624.

Opposite: The interior of the house of Lee Huncharoen on Samui island shows how the roof structure and underside of the tiles are left exposed. Note also the attention given to good ventilation. Pictures of the royal family, the Buddha, monks and family ancestors are hung high up where the walls reach the beginning of the roof.

Right: The sitting room and the bedroom within the new palace of the the governor of Patthalung, situated in Lumpa sub-district, Muang district. Today the compound is in the care of the Fine Arts Department. Note the large posts and wide boards which run across the width of the house.

Far left: A typical Southern-style *ruen krueng pook*. Several different materials are used in its construction: the walls are of woven split bamboo, the thatched roof can be of *Imperata* or *Vertiveria* grass, or nipa palm bound together with rattan or *liphao* vines. In the Central region such houses are referred to as *ruen khat thae*.

Left: A *ruen krueng pook* style granary. The walls are of split bamboo woven in a distinctive herringbone pattern.

A Southern style *ruen krueng sab* on Samui island belonging to Lee Huncharoen. Note the widely projecting lower roof to prevent rain blowing in.

Vernacular houses

As stated above, traditional Thai houses, whether in the Central region, the Northeast or the South can be divided into two categories: *ruen krueng pook* and *ruen krueng sab*.

In the South the components for making the *ruen krueng pook* are readily available such as bamboo, nipa palm for thatch, or coconut trees for certain structural components. The house posts and roof structure are usually of medium-strength or hardwood trees. In some areas *laocha-own* (*Oncosperma tigillaria*), a readily available type of palm is widely used once it has been trimmed. Roof coverings come from a variety of sources such as thatch of *ya kha* (*Imperata aundinacea*) or *faek* (*Vertiveria*) grass and a variety of palm leaves such as *taan* (*Borassus flabellifera*), *laan* (*Corypha lecomtei*), *jaak* (*Nipa fruticans*) and *sakhu* (*Metroxylon sagus*). Split bamboo, nipa palm or pandanus woven matting are made into wall and partition panels. Binding materials come from rattan, *lumtheng* vines, *liphao* (*Lygodium flexuosum*) vines, the fibres pulled from the central vein of *taan* and *laan* palm leaves, and young bamboo trunks crushed and twisted into rope. Any joint that will receive significant weight, for example, joints of main posts and beams will receive supplementary binding. The *khat lae* (known as *khat thae* in the Central region) or tourniquet technique is employed, with the middle of the rope placed under the beam and its two ends tightly twisted

Right: A *ruen krueng pook* belonging to a fisherman's family. The underneath of the house has become a storage place for fishing baskets.

Far right: This twin-roofed Muslim house has the hallmark roof finial decorations and delicate fretwork railings on the verandah.

around the post. The stick or rod used for twisting, or *look lae*, is left permanently in place at the joint.

Nowadays it is very difficult to find a good example of a *ruen krueng pook* because modern building materials such as nails, corrugated iron and concrete footings are used with increasing frequency. Not only are they more durable but they do not require a knowledge of traditional building techniques. Nevertheless, traditional building methods for making roof coverings and erecting matting panels are still maintained in many villages, such as in the Sea Gypsy villages of Phuket and other villages in the provinces of Pattani and Narathiwat.

As the family grows and prospers there is a need for larger, stronger and more permanent dwellings. The *ruen krueng sab* was conceived to serve this need. Such a house is made of wood, carefully constructed to the desired proportions. The building techniques employed are also more complex and elaborate, with the use of tenon, mortise and dowel joints. A house of this type cannot be put together in a few days by the owner with the help of a few friends. The materials and stylistic refinements are expensive and require specialists in particular fields. Such a house will therefore reflect the occupants' economic position.

The house may use a variety of different woods selected according to the functional requirements of each component of the house. For example, posts are chosen from hardwoods (*saya, khiem* and *loompau*)

trimmed into balk posts with the top slightly smaller than the bottom. Medium-strength woods and hardwoods (*saya, khiem, loompau, tamsao, takhien* and *yang* trees) are chosen for the roof structure. In some areas mature nipa palm logs are used for tie beams, joists, crossbeams, purlins, latches and lathes. Partitions are made from *yang, thang* and *saya*, while the floor uses split bamboo or wooden planks.

For the roof covering, ceramic roof tiles were already popular in the reign of King Rama V. They were initially introduced by Chao Phraya Yommarat (Pan Sukhum), the governor of Nakhon Si Thammarat around 1898, when he noted that the town looked shabby because the roofs of the houses were of poor materials. At the time it was considered to be most inappropriate for commoners to build houses to a similar or better standard than those of the nobility and royalty. Nevertheless, Chao Phraya Yommarat suggested that all local houses should be constructed with wooden walls and tiled roofs, an idea that was possibly derived from the availability of both materials and technology in the area, following the settlement of a Chinese community who were engaged in trade and mining. They had already built Chinese-style houses with tiled roofs. However, instead of Chinese tiles, thin terracotta tiles of 15-18 x 22-28 cm and 6-8 cm thick were used. The tile had a lip at one end to hook onto the laths while the other end was cut into a triangular shape. This type of roof tile has remained popu-

Right: The interior of a roof covered with kite-shaped tiles. Note the carvings at the ends of the posts supporting the cross beams [purlins]. (Lee Huncharoen house, Samui)

Far right: The interior roof structure of a typical *ruen krueng sab* house found throughout Southern Thailand.

Above: A simple concrete base supports one of the wooden posts at Wat Choltara Singhae in Tak Bai district, Narathiwat province.

Opposite: Inside the main room of the new palace of Phraya Abhai Boriraksha in Patthalung. Although certain aspects are similar to Central Thai houses, the eaves come down much lower to protect the house from the constant Southern rains.

lar to this day in Nakhon Si Thammarat and other lower Southern provinces. They are produced in the areas around Koh Yor of Songkhla and Pattani, often in small workshops in the grounds of local houses.

Among the upper Southern provinces, cement tiles are more popular and the Songkhla-style terracotta tiles are used in certain areas only. Another innovation over the last few decades has been the use of the relatively cheap corrugated iron sheets which keep out the rain better than natural materials, are more long lasting and require no labour. Unfortunately, they are not nearly as aesthetically pleasing as tiles.

In the South the *ruen krueng sab* can be divided into two distinct categories: Thai Buddhist and Thai Muslim houses. While their construction and form may derive from similar aims such as mitigating the effects of the strong and constant rain, or of taking advantage of sea breezes, both are a reflection of the occupants' differing cultural backgrounds. The structure, layout and details of these houses will be discussed in the following sections.

Southern Thai Buddhist houses

In general, Thai Buddhist houses share the general features of houses in the Central region as most of the Southern provinces were previously dependencies of the Central Thai kingdoms, especially Ayutthaya. Ties between the two regions were maintained in times of peace and war. However the Southern Thais have

modified the Central Thai houses to suit their geographical and climatic conditions, thereby creating the distinctively unique house forms of the South.

As in the Central region, the structural elements of the house are put together first to form a rigid frame to which other components – roof coverings, floors and walls – are added. Structural stability is achieved through these interconnected parts. As a response to the high humidity and heavy rainfall in the South, house posts are not sunk into post holes in the ground, but rather rest on *teen sao* (footings), which are made from a block of hardwood, stone or, latterly, mostly cement. *Teen sao* not only solve the problems of waterlogged sites and termites, but they also facilitate house-moving as the main posts do not have to be dug out of the ground. Nevertheless there are still a few older houses in Pattani that have their house posts buried in the ground. As these are believed to be the oldest houses in the area, it suggests that originally the posts were sunk in the ground and the adoption of the *teen sao* is a later modification.

In comparison to the Central region, the pitch of the Southern house roof is lower and the structure is less exposed, to cope with the year-round winds and storms. The *panlom* (a windbreak on the gable) is made of stucco in fishtail style instead of wood; it sometimes stretches the whole length of the roof ridge. A low-pitched roof and inward-slanting walls reduce the uplift on the end tiles and protect the area under-

Left: One of the characteristics of Southern architecture is the use of colour on various features such as on these two *hong* (swans) associated with good fortune. Here they form supports for the rafters.

Right: Four ventilation panels in Thai Buddhist houses, typical of southern architecture. These examples all come from Samui island. At bottom is stucco detailing from the end of a roof ridge.

The panel above this door has a pierced section on the right and the painting of a *khojasee,* a mythical beast on the left. In Thai Buddhist houses representations of animals were acceptable but in Muslim houses images of the human form or animals are not allowed.

neath the house from rain. Small openings at the top of the walls provide cross ventilation.

For coastal areas such as the islands of Phuket and Samui, the wet climate makes an open verandah impractical and a single house with no verandah has become popular. The Central region style of a twin house with connecting corridor is modified to have walls or awnings to protect the verandah from rain.

The verandah floors in a Southern house are of durable wood from the *khiem* tree. The planks are 2-3 5-7 cm thick and 24-30 cm wide and with a 2-4 cm gap between each plank. Nails are not use to lay the floorboards because they would create indentations that trap rainwater and cause wood rot. The houses are raised high enough above the ground to allow people to walk underneath as well as providing protection from flash floods and unwanted animals, such as snakes, centipedes and termites.

House walls are made of overlapping horizontal planks. Old houses built during the reigns of Kings Rama III, IV and V have plastered bamboo mat walls, which can still be seen on the *kuti* of Wat Machimavas and Wat Khu Tao in Songkhla province.

The pitched roofs of Thai Buddhist houses usually have blocked gables made of plastered bamboo or wood frames. Often the gables are covered with overlapping wood panels spread out in a fan-shaped design called *lai rasamee phra arthit* (the sun ray motif). A popular style is a hipped or Manila roof, which is

Characteristic features of Southern roofs are the decoration of the gable end and the finial above the gable. Gable ends frequently have the sunburst motif which can vary in form as these pictures show. The finials on the top of the gable can be made of wood, stucco or metal. More unusual is the praying figure surrounded by foliage (below left). Gingerbread fretwork is another frequently found detail of Southern architectural.

influenced by the Thai Muslim house style, as is the use of stucco ornamentation on the roof ridges or the hips. A synthesis of the two house forms can be seen in the *kuti* of Wat Choltara Singhae of Tak Bai district, Narathiwat province. However, despite such stylistic borrowings the houses can still be clearly distinguished by such features as their different layout and decorative detailing.

A unique feature of the Thai Buddhist house is the use of colour in the interior decoration. This feature is particularly popular with the *kuti*. The designs used consist of a variety of human, animal, and vegetal, as well as Chinese motifs. They appear mainly on wooden frames separating the *keoy* (platform) from the interior of the house. They are used in combination with ornately carved fretwood pieces to decorate the posts and ceilings.

Because Southern houses have few windows, wooden ventilation panels are inserted at various places in the walls, and around or above the windows. These are carved with intricate fretwork designs with geometric, vegetal, or classical Thai motifs. Such exquisite work found in both Buddhist and Muslim houses is a folk art form unique to the South.

A distinctive feature of a Thai Buddhist house, which is shared with those in the other regions, is its layout derived from the tradition of having married daughters living with the parents, whether under the same roof or in an adjacent house, which is an

The *kuti* of the abbot of Wat Choltara Singhae in Tak Bai, Narathiwat. This imposing, two-storey wooden building combines elements of Muslim, Buddhist and Chinese architecture. The edge of the roof has fretwork decoration, the hip of the terracotta tiled roof has stucco detailing and the gable end has an intricate design.

Right: Diverse pierced fretwork designs are found on the ventilation panels of various Thai Buddhist houses.

Below right: The ventilation panels above the doors of the abbot's *kuti* in Wat Choltara Singhae are painted with praying deities on lotus flowers.

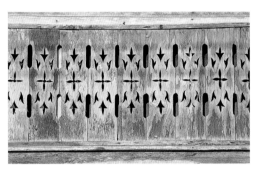

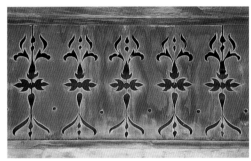

extension of the main house. This has led to the development of twin houses with connecting corridors and clustered houses, in which two to three adjacent houses are grouped together.

The house plan also reflects the tradition of co-residence; all family members residing under the same roof, while daughters and sons occupy separate sleeping quarters. The house plan consists of a room for the parents and an open sleeping hall for the sons. If there are daughters, the house is partitioned off to create a separate room for them. Visitors usually sleep in the open hall or on the verandah. Every house will have at least one open hall. In a three-room house the central room is usually the open hall.

A Thai Buddhist house is usually entered from the connecting corridor between the two adjacent houses or from a deck, which runs parallel to one side of the house. The entrance is flanked on both sides by solid walls, which also form the outer panels of the verandah. The stairway, a brick structure with few steps, leads to the lowest platform of the house. In an ordinary house the entrance is a simple solid door, with or without portal, while a monk's quarters or a wealthy house usually has an entrance with a Chinese-style brick portal, solid brick walls or walls with insets of open fretwork ceramic tiles enclosing the terrace. In most houses the buildings are laid out around a central rectangular courtyard, whose floor is usually paved with terracotta tiles 33 cm square and 4 cm thick.

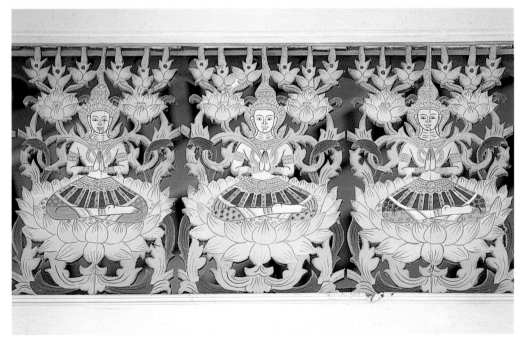

Opposite: The sitting area in Yaring palace is surrounded on three sides by typically Muslim-style rounded windows with coloured glass infills. Above are venitlation panels.

Right: The dining room section of the main room in Yaring palace, Pattani. The ventilation panels have a pattern of pierced foliage. The furniture is typically arranged around the walls.

Below right: A twin-gabled house in Yaring.

Thai Muslim houses

These houses are mainly found in the border provinces of the South: Pattani, Yala, Narathiwat and Satun. Since ancient times, Pattani has been the centre of Muslim culture, while Songkhla has been dominated by Buddhist culture with a blend of Chinese influence.

Geographical factors have had a strong influence on the basic features of both Thai Buddhist and Thai Muslim houses, such as the use of high posts on footings and ventilation openings above the windows, below the eaves and in certain wall panels. It is thus cultural factors that distinguish a Thai Muslim house from its Buddhist counterpart.

A Thai Muslim house is generally larger in size and tends to be built in a twin or clustered-house style. It differs from a Buddhist house in that the verandah is entirely covered, as the houses (usually between two-five, but maybe more) are built very close with continuous roofs and floors. This layout is a result of the preference on the part of Muslim parents for having their children living nearby. However, each family has its own cooking area. Nowadays houses are usually built for a nuclear family but nevertheless their layout is that of a double-roofed or continuous-roofed structure to accommodate the grandparents.

Shade in Thai Muslim house compounds is created by fruit trees such as banana, coconut and cashew. Sometimes a low wooden platform is erected under the trees as a place for taking meals, weaving mats, drying

The panels above the window are pierced with foliage fretwork.

fish, etc. Ornamental plants are placed in pots in front of the house, turtle dove cages will hang on the terrace and a small water jar stands next to the stairway for washing one's feet before ascending to the house. Also found in some courtyards are an artesian well for general use and an open-air bathing area. The area under the house is used as a shelter for animals.

In front of a Thai Muslim house is a stairway ascending to a covered verandah, which is a communal area for general activities. There are benches along the railings for resting and receiving visitors. The verandah gives access to the interior of the house, which consists of a hall and a bedroom whose floor level is raised higher. At the back of the house on a lower level is the kitchen, while the washing area, next to the back stairway, is one level lower still. In general, the wooden floorboards are laid along the length of the house. In the kitchen a certain section of the floor is made of widely-spaced split bamboo to serve as a washing area.

The hall in the interior of a Thai Muslim house is an important area used for all kinds of social and religious activities, as well as for rites of passage such as the birth of a family member, a wedding, or a funeral. The bedroom is situated at one corner of the hall, its partitioning walls being just above head height. The arrangement of the different areas of the house on varying levels reflects its functional hierarchy. Muslim houses have exposed ceilings and relatively few pieces of furniture as, like elsewhere in Thailand,

their occupants generally favour sitting on the floor. Usually there will be a display cabinet with glass doors containing family treasures and other odds and ends.

The windows normally extend to the floor. The outer walls are wood panels while the interior partitions are made from carved fretwork or balustraded panels 70-80 cm high. Intricately carved fretwork panels are inserted above the windows and along the top of the walls under the eaves. The quality of the overall workmanship will reflect the relative position and affluence of the house owner.

A further aspect of the house which may be regarded as Southern folk art are wall panels made from woven bamboo slats and mats, mostly popular in Narathiwat. Yet another type of wall covering found in very old Thai Muslim houses are the overlapping horizontal boards and wooden panels in combination with intricate fretwork or carved wood, reflecting Malaysian influence. There are various patterns of panel arrangement some of which are similar to the Central region panels.

The most unique feature of a Thai Muslim house is its roof forms, which fall into three styles: gabled (*maelae*), hipped (*lima*), and Manila (*blanor*) roof. Often more than one style of roof is combined on a single house. The pitch-gabled roof shows Central Thai influence, but the addition of the *peek nok* (soffit) is evidently a Malay feature. The hipped roof is a unique Southern architectural style found in all provinces, especially in Pattani. The word *lima* or five in Arabic

Left: A window carved with motifs reflecting the influence of Chinese architecture.

Below: A Thai Muslim house with a *blanor* roof. The windows open down to the floor. Yarang district, Pattani.

Bottom: A twin house in Pattani with *blanor* roof and windows to floor level.

The pierced arch above the entrance porch to the house of the Kamnan Sahoh Doloh Al-Hufree, in Yamu sub-district, Yaring district, clearly shows the influence of Muslim architecture.

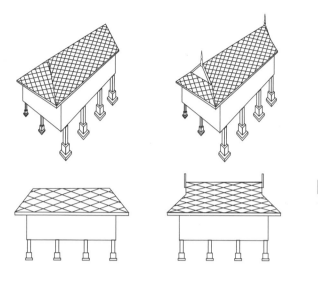

The three roof styles found on
Thai Muslim houses:
1. *Banya* or Lima style roof.
2. Manila or *blanor* hip-gabled roof.
3. Gabled or *maelae* roof.

Above: A Thai style house with
a *banya* style roof on Yor island,
Songkhla. Note the absence
of windows in favour of simple
openings for ventilation.

Right: A wide variety of carvings
can be found on the panels of
some Muslim houses.

refers to the five ridges of the roof and is a symbolic
expression of the five saints of Islam. The Manila or
blanor roof is a hip-gabled roof whose gable edges are
elaborately decorated with carved fretwork panels
or stucco. The word *blanor* refers to the Dutch and
indicates an architectural influence from Indonesia.

Just as with the Thai Buddhist house, a rice granary
forms an important part of a Thai Muslim compound.
It is usually located in an auspicious location at the
side or back and to the east or west of the house. Such
locations are believed to confer fertility and an overflowing stock of rice. The granary is a rectangular
building of moderate size, raised high above the
ground. It has a gabled or hipped roof with nipa palm
thatch or terracotta tiles. The bamboo slats or corru-
gate iron granary walls have no windows and there is
only one entrance via a ladder leaning against the
platform at the front, where containers for rice can be
rested before unloading.

Each house has an artesian well, which is also a
bathing area as Thai Muslims do not bathe in the house.
When houses are built in a cluster, the residents may
share a collective well. The well is usually located in an
open space in front of or at the side of the house.
Sometimes a roof is built over it, or it may be screened
off for privacy using either bamboo or nipa palm.

Attractive details are a feature of Thai Muslim
house. Apart from the beautiful fretwork, the roof ridge
is decorated with floral designs in stucco or metal.

In this large house belonging to Kamnan Abdul Romay Kordor in Yarang district, Pattani, the well is situated within the open court.

Right: The diverse gable finials are one of the most distinctive features of Southern Muslim architecture.

Far right: This Muslim house in Sai Buri district, Pattani, belonging to Adul Na Sai Buri, has a double-gabled roof with intricate fretwork on the ventilation panels.

Above: A twin-gabled Muslim house with a projecting gabled porch covering the stairway. Banana and other fruit trees have been planted in the garden.

Far left: The interior of a Thai Muslim house. A turtle dove is suspended from one of the beams. The geometrically patterned ventilation panels filter the light through. As with most Thai families there are no sofas or chairs as everyone prefers to sit on the floor.

Left: A typical Muslim kitchen.

The gables and the apex are decorated with carved wood, stucco, metal plates or painting. Sometimes the gable is constructed of overlapping wood panels, fanned out in a *rasmi* (sunburst) design similar to the Central region house. The eaves and the tops of the walls or windows are decorated with carved fretwork panels or pierced metal plates, which sometimes have the appearance of lace. These decorative motifs are influenced by Malay aesthetics; other designs reflect Chinese influence. Ventilation slots above the windows may also use Arabic calligraphy in praise of Allah, as it is believed that the presence of these sacred words will bring good fortune to the residents. The openings can be square or arched and divided into slots in the ray or petal design.

The balustrades are made of decorative laths of carved wood in geometric or lace-like designs. In the past the footing for the house posts were decorated with relief stucco moldings, but today these are being replaced by plain cement footings.

Decorative motifs in Thai Muslim houses can be divided into three main categories: geometric, natural (floral and vegetal), and calligraphic (Arabic phrases from the Koran or the names of esteemed religious leaders). The prohibition against the representation of human and animal forms is a notable difference between a Thai Buddhist and a Thai Muslim house.

The forms of Muslim houses vary depending on their function and the wealth of the family. They encompass everything from the spacious and lavishly decorated house of a rich family, to a two-story shop-house. Such shop-houses are usually on the same level as, or only one step above, the street. Some consist of a long structure parallel to the road, divided into small rooms similar to a row house. Despite its utilitarian purpose the shop-house roof and ventilation openings may be beautifully decorated. Fishermen and farmers generally have simple houses made of local materials, with walls of bamboo slats or woven palm matting, and gabled or hipped roofs of terracotta tile or corrugated iron.

Above: The designs on ventilation panels above doors and windows may be derived from foliage or flowers.

Below: Apart from floral motifs, geometric designs are found on Muslim houses, whether above the windows or in the form of balustrades.

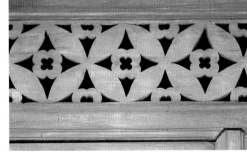

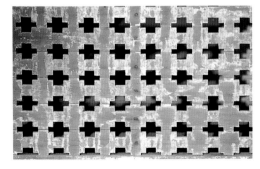

Opposite: The New Palace of the governor of Patthalung, seen from outside the courtyard.

Right: A wayside pavilion in Thai Muslim style on the raod between Narathiwat and Tak Bai.

Traditional Beliefs

Above: The frame of the house can be moved by getting neighbours and friends to lend a hand.

Right: A simple Southern house with a tiled roof. Here the house is raised only a few inches off the ground on stubby, concrete footings.

As with other regions of Thailand, traditional beliefs play an important role in determining vernacular house forms. As with the functional and decorative details, there are similarities and differences between the Thai Buddhist and Thai Muslim houses

Thai Buddhist houses

The location is regulated by such factors as the direction of the sun, wind, and rain. A belief exists that a house should not be built *kwang tawan* (facing north or south) as it will bring grave adversity to the residents. Thus the houses are generally built facing east or west. In addition, facing north or south would situate the house in the direction of the prevailing wind and rain, which could be dangerous during a heavy storm. However, the exception to this rule is the rice granary, which is normally built *kwang tawan* so that it can receive as much heat as possible in order to dry the stored grain.

Another belief found elsewhere in Thailand is that which prohibits the building of a two-story house as it is feared that a person of lower status might go upstairs and so be above his or her superior. In the past Southerners, especially men, usually wore amulets and other sacred items around their neck. Such objects are considered to lose their magical power if the owner's head is crossed by a woman and, clearly, a two-story house means that such a possibility is always present.

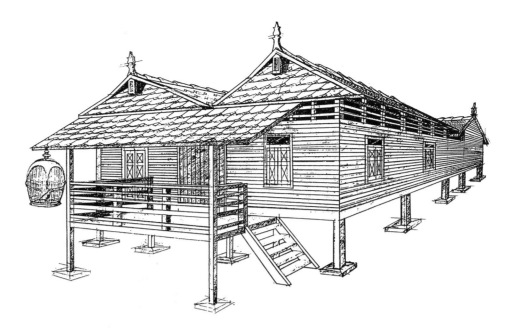

Above right: A line drawing of a typical Muslim house with ventilation panels below the eaves, finials on the gable and a dove cage hanging near the terrace.

Below: A line drawing illustrating the various components of a Thai Muslim house.

The belief that the verandah and the bedroom should not be on the same level, relates to Thai idea regarding social hierarchy and the tradition of paying respect to one's elders. The different floor levels ensure that the younger members of the family can sit at a lower level than their elders. The shelf for sacred objects must be placed in a high place in the bedroom.

Thai Muslim houses

In the past there were many rituals connected with house erection which are probably of Brahmin origin and derive from the period when the South was largely Buddhist. Such customs still endured after the majority of the population converted to Islam. The customs described below are still observed today to a greater or lesser extent.

The house site and the area to the east and west should be flat, with the area to the north slightly higher and the area to the south slightly lower. The soil should be pale, red or yellow with a sweet smell and a bitter taste.

The house should face east or west, with east being the most favourable. It should not be built *kwang tawan* as this will bring ill health to the occupants. The front of the house often faces the road, while the bedroom should be on the west. The rice granary, which reflects the wealth and standing of the family, is an important structure. It is believed that building it to the east or the south within the compound will ensure that the granary is always full.

The house owner must seek an auspicious time to start building from a knowledgeable person such as the Imam. Fridays are not suitable for building as that is day when Muslims go to the mosque. Auspicious days are considered to be Sundays, Tuesdays and Thursdays. Inauspicious days are Wednesdays and Saturdays. In addition houses are not generally built during the waning cycle of the moon.

An average house has six posts which are all erected on the same day. However, there can be as many as 12. The middle post on the northern side is the main

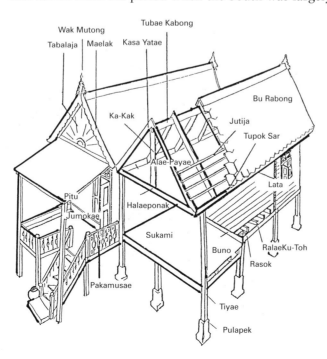

The stages in the construction of a Thai Muslim house.

1. The posts and various components are laid out on the site.
2. The *sao ek* is in position.
3. The remaining posts and floor beams are in position.
4. The roof structure goes on.
5. The *pae* and tiles are placed.
6. Once the roof has gone on, the floor may be laid.
7. The wall panels, windows and ceiling is added.
8. The terrace section is built.
9. The kitchen is added at the back.
10. The stairs are last.

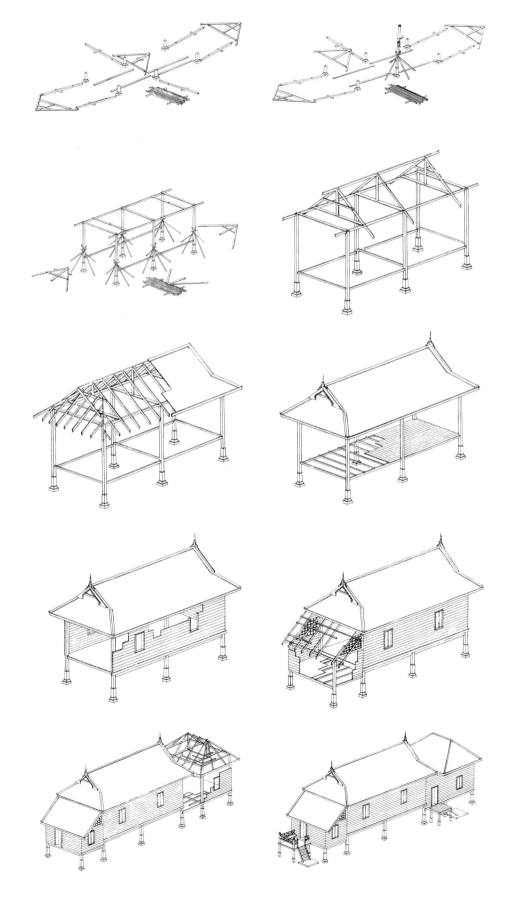

one – the *sao ek*, known locally as *tieng seu ru*. In the past a coin to the value of one *satang* was attached to the base of this post but today a one *baht* coin is used instead. On the day the posts are erected sticky and saffron rice, known locally as *poo lod kun yid* are prepared for the guests. The number of steps must be uneven: such as three, five or seven. Steps with an even number of treads as seen as being for ghosts and bring misfortune to the inhabitants.

Usually a significant day in the religious calendar is chosen for moving in, such as Friday with the auspicious time being at some point in the morning. Religious leaders and neighbours are asked to come and give and receive blessing in order to bring good luck to the family. A meal will also be served. In addition Arab months are popular for house-warming ceremonies such as the month of Ramadan or the month in which Mohammed was born, otherwise known as the Muwlid month. In this case not only will a house-warming ceremony be carried out but a Muwlid ceremony as well.

The interior of the building is oriented around praying to Mecca, something which needs to be done five times a day. The praying area, which must be within the main house, needs to be screened off to stop people walking by and must face west. The stages in the construction of a Thai Muslim house are very similar to those found in the Central region as may be seen from the drawings.

Religious Buildings

Religious buildings frequently reflect outside influences, especially the dominant architectural styles of the capital city. However, religious structures in the South have been able to develop a unique vernacular architectural style, as may be seen at Wat Phra Barommathat Chaiya of Surat Thani, or at Wat Mahathat Voraviharn in Nakhon Si Thammarat and in the various *kuti*, pavilions, bell towers, reliquary monuments and mosques.

Buddhist temples

Buddhist temples in the South are influenced by the Central style of architecture, especially in the forms of the *ubosot* and *viharn*. The Southern *chedi* and their *plong chanai* (the moldings at the top) are renowned for their graceful curves. Most Buddhist buildings are decorated with stucco, paintings, fretwork and carved wood in intricate designs. Good examples may be found at Wat Suwankhiri, Wat Machimavas, Wat Laem Pau and Wat Khu Tao in Songkhla province; Wat Choltara Singhae in Narathiwat province; and Wat Yanikaram and Wat Mahingsa in Pattani. The decorative designs are a combination of Thai, Chinese, geometric and floral motifs. Muslim influences can also be detected in certain religious buildings. Notable examples include the adoption of the hipped or Manila roof and its various adornments, fretwork and carved panels, the use of paintings and the pointed Koh Yor terracotta roof tiles.

Top: This monk's *kuti* is a twin-gabled house with terracotta tiles standing on concrete footings.

Above: This pavilion in the grounds of Wat Ta Miraum in Patthalung, has a stepped roof and painted and pierced walls.

Above and right: Details of the pavilion in the grounds of Wat Ta Miraum show a mix of architectural styles as well as a dramatic colour scheme.

The pavilion of the landing stage on the Tak Bai River at Wat Choltara Singhae has a receding stepped roof with elaborate finial and roof ridge decoration.